In praise of Gina

'Thank you so much Gina Ford. You and your books are truly heaven sent'

'Without your books I do not know what I would have done. Your advice has meant that I have a fantastic, happy little boy and I actually look forward to the next challenge he may bring as I know where the answer to any problem lies!'

'I was so happy with *The Contented Little Baby Book* that I also bought your next book *The Contented Toddler Years*. This book is also fantastic and I'm looking forward to putting into practice your advice on potty training amongst other things.'

'I would like to express my gratitude for your book. It has been an absolute saviour and my best friend since I started my little boy on your routine when he was 10 weeks old. He is nearly nine months old now and everyone always says of him "what a happy contented little baby!"'

'From day one of Macey's return home from Hospital we put her into Gina's routine and have never looked back. Everyone comments on Macey and what an unbelievably happy and contented baby she is . . . Thank you, Gina, for your books and the enjoyment and confidence they have given us.'

'Gina transformed our son into the happiest, "easiest" baby, that we could have wished for. Her knowledge and professionalism is astounding; she has answers to every question – and they really work.'

'My friends tell me that it is not "normal" for a baby to be as happy and well behaved as my daughter. It certainly seems to be normal for "Gina's babies".'

'I followed Gina's advice with my first baby, who happily fell into the routine from the beginning. Friends said that I was lucky that she was such an easy baby and that I would not be so lucky the second time around. When I gave birth I followed the routines again, and although it was hard work with two children under two, I am proud to say that they are both very contented and calm children. Having happy and contented children is not down to luck – it is defiantly down to Gina.'

The
Contented
Toddler
Years

The
Contented
Toddler
Years

Gina Ford

Vermilion
LONDON

To my beloved mother and best friend
in blessed remembrance of all her wisdom and the very special
love, support and encouragement she always gave me.
She taught me the difference between right and wrong
and how always to march to the beat of my own drum.

12

First published in the UK as *From Contented Baby to Confident Child*
in 2000 by Vermilion, an imprint of Ebury Publishing
This edition published by Vermilion in 2006

Ebury Publishing is a Random House Group company

The Random House Group Limited Reg. No. 954009

Addresses for companies within the Random House Group can be found at
www.randomhouse.co.uk

A CIP catalogue record for this book is available from the British Library

The Random House Group Limited supports The Forest Stewardship
Council® (FSC®), the leading international forest-certification organisation.
Our books carrying the FSC label are printed on FSC®-certified paper.
FSC is the only forest-certification scheme supported by the leading
environmental organisations, including Greenpeace. Our
paper procurement policy can be found at
www.randomhouse.co.uk/environment

Printed and bound in Great Britain by Clays Ltd, St Ives plc

ISBN 9780091912666

Copies are available at special rates for bulk orders.
Contact the sales development team on 020 7840 8487 or visit
www.booksforpromotion.co.uk for more information.

To buy books by your favourite authors and register for offers, visit
www.randomhouse.co.uk

Please note that conversions to imperial weights and measures are
suitable equivalents and not exact.

The information given in this book should not be treated as a
substitute for qualified medical advice; always consult a medical practi-
tioner. Neither the author nor the publisher can be held responsible for
any loss or claim arising out of the use, or misuse, of the suggestions
made or the failure to take medical advice.

Contents

Acknowledgements

In writing this book, I have relied enormously on the continual feedback from, and the constant contact with the hundreds of parents who have shared their babies with me. It has been a great honour that they have continued to involve me in their family life for many years after I first went to help care for their babies. I would like to thank all those parents and in particular the following whose constant encouragement, enthusiasm and suggestions have been invaluable: Kay and Simon Brewer, Verity and Michael Chamber, Janetta and Keith Hodgson, Jackie and Andrew Marr, Sabrina and Danny Masri, Ameila and Neil Mendoza, Juliette and Alistair Scott, Helen and David Sherbourne, and Catherine and Rupert Vaughan Williams.

A very special thank you to my Aunt Jean and Uncle Dan, and my cousins Ann Clough and Sheila Eskdale for your love, continued support and encouragement and for helping look after my darling Molly. I would also like to thank Jane Revell, Carla Flodden Flint for their special friendship and emotional support.

I owe a further debt of thanks to my agent Emma Todd for her continued support and encouragement with my writing. And to everyone at Random House, in particular my publisher Fiona MacIntyre and editor Imogen Fortes. Also to Becky Bagnell, a huge thank you for helping me transform my manuscript into an understandable and readable text.

A very special thank you to my personal editors Dawn Fozard and Gill MacCaulay who have not only helped me hugely with my books and website, but whose emotional support, encouragement and friendship are a constant inspiration to me.

Frances Howard-Brown who joined the Contentedbaby.com team in November 2005 deserves a very big thank you. Each month she deals with the hundreds of questions and emails from readers of my books and members of the website.

Rory Jenkins of Embado.com is responsible for creating Contentedbaby.com; he deserves a special mention. His technical skills have helped create a wonderful supportive online community for parents of Contented babies around the world.

Finally, a very special thank you to all parents of contented babies who continue to update me on your baby's development over the years. It is that feedback that has helped me make this book possible.

The Toddler Years – an Introduction

I am often curious to know how parents envisage their children in the years ahead. Hopes and expectations vary enormously, but one ambition that most parents share is that their baby will grow up to be a healthy, happy and confident adult. During the growing years, parents assume that their child will develop many skills and attributes including, they hope, the ability to play contentedly with other children, the courage to face new challenges, politeness and generosity of spirit. It is a long list of expectations for a small human being, but it is what parents dream of and, to some extent, expect of their baby.

I have yet to hear a parent say, 'I don't mind if my baby turns out to be a spoilt toddler and a selfish, bad-mannered child.' Of course, even with skilled parenting and excellent routines, all children misbehave at times. Frustrations will arise and tantrums will result, but this is normal and should be anticipated. Yet, at toddler groups or in the playground, many of us will have met a child who is unusually difficult to handle and whose behaviour is often challenging.

These children were not born like that, so what's gone wrong? The blame is often laid on the parents. The older generation may declare that today's children are over-indulged and that a tougher line should be taken from day one. If, however, we consider the views of psychologists, and those involved in child development, the authoritarian approach is often thought to be the cause of insecurity in children and unhappiness in adults.

I do not profess to have all the answers on how to help your contented baby become a confident child. However, over the years, my hands-on experience of working and living with families all over the world has taught me a great deal about what works and what doesn't. I have observed the behaviour, both good and bad, of hundreds of toddlers and young children and also considered the different ways in which parents deal with their children's discipline. Some will follow their own parents' strict, autocratic approach; others have a more liberal style, taking time to talk, explain and reason with their children. Regardless of approach, parents can get very distraught about their children's difficult behaviour, leading to feelings of guilt, frustration and ultimately desperation.

I have written this book with the aim of enhancing parents' knowledge and understanding of their toddler's needs, desires and behaviour. With this wisdom, the different characteristics of each developmental stage can be anticipated, and any difficulties can be addressed with calmness and confidence. The toddler years present a steep learning curve for both parent and child, and a deeper insight into the challenges and delights of this special period will enrich your experience. But it is not rocket science. It is my belief that the simple combination of a safe and happy home, a healthy diet, a good routine, encouragement and love will successfully result in your baby becoming a confident child.

1
The Second Year
(12 to 24 months)

A child learns more between the ages of one and three years than at any other time in his life. The learning process often ends up in tears of frustration through not being understood, and sheer exhaustion from having to learn so many different things at the same time. This time often sees the arrival of a new baby, which adds the fear of abandonment and feelings of jealousy to the very long list of emotions with which the toddler has to cope.

Listed below are just a few of the main skills and challenges a toddler has to deal with in his second year:

- Learning to become more physically independent – walking and climbing
- Learning to make his needs understood – talking
- Learning how to make choices about what to eat and how to feed himself
- Learning to undress and eventually to dress himself
- Learning how to integrate with other toddlers – playing and sharing

Managing your toddler

Creating a safe, happy and relaxed environment will help increase the toddler's confidence during this critical stage of mental, physical and emotional development. However, there will be times when he becomes so challenged that he finds it difficult to cope. Therefore, it is essential that parents set very clear limits and boundaries for dealing with any difficult behaviour caused by their toddler's frustration.

For example, as adults, if we choose to learn how to drive, we place ourselves in the hands of a driving instructor. A good teacher makes the rules and sets the limits, and provides us with a sound framework so that we can learn to drive successfully. He will also show great patience and tolerance as we learn to master both the mental and physical skills needed to drive properly and safely. He will not ridicule or punish us when we make a mistake. However, he would take over the control of the car if we were about to make a mistake that could have serious consequences.

It is important that parents show the same patience and tolerance when their toddler is learning the numerous new skills with which he is faced, and, when necessary, be prepared to take charge if things appear to be getting out of control. There is very little room for punishment at this stage of child development.

Toddlers, if they are to grow into confident and happy children, need to learn with the minimum of frustration. As adults and teachers it is our responsibility to ensure that we provide our children with a sound framework, and a clear set of rules and limits that help the toddler face the challenge, not that challenge the toddler. The right environment, along with your help and encouragement, will make it easier for your toddler to master the many skills he has to learn during toddlerhood.

Q During her first year my 18-month-old daughter was such an easy-going baby. She would spend up to an hour or more crawling around and playing happily with her toys, allowing me to get all my chores done. Over the last few months she has become more and more demanding, and now I find it impossible to get any work done in the morning. Every time she is faced with a challenge that she has difficulty mastering she becomes extremely frustrated and tearful, saying, 'Mummy do it'. In the beginning I always used to end up showing her how to do it, as I hated seeing her so upset. But we have now reached a situation where I can't leave her alone for even a few minutes to do a simple jigsaw puzzle or play with her Lego before she is getting upset and demanding my attention. My husband says that I have been too soft with her, pandering to her every need, and that she is attention seeking and must learn to work things out for herself. When I leave her to work things out she usually ends up even more upset, having a mega tantrum, and I end up doing it anyway.

I am doing more and more household chores in the evening, which means my husband and I spend hardly any time together. I'm getting more and more depressed trying to keep my daughter and my husband happy and fit in the housework, yet not really succeeding at anything. To make matters worse, I now find that I'm pregnant. We have no close relatives at hand to help out and I'm at my wits' end trying to cope.

A Once they pass their first birthday and enter toddlerhood, the majority of babies become more demanding and need much more attention. Although they are striving towards independence physically, mentally and emotionally, they go through a stage where they need a lot more reassurance and attention. While I agree with your husband that it is important that your daughter learns to work things out for herself, it is unfair to expect her to do so without some help. It is important that you are very supportive during this frustrating stage in your daughter's development. When she is trying to work out solutions for a new task or skill, it is important that you help guide her but at the same time do not actually solve the problem for her.

For example if she is struggling to find the right piece of puzzle or the right Lego brick, reduce the number of pieces she has to choose from to two, making the choice easier but not actually choosing for her. This principle can apply to any game, task or skill that she is attempting to learn.

When she gets it right, give her lots of praise and hugs. When she get it wrong, show her which one it should have been but still get her to do the task herself.

During this stage it might also be a good idea to have a change of routine in the morning. Toddlers of this age wake up and are raring to go. Perhaps it would be better to take your daughter out for a short walk in the park before you attempt to do any chores. Alternatively, get her to help you with the chores. Most toddlers of this age love to assist and they can learn a lot about colours and numbers when helping to load the washing machine or dust two of the chairs while Mummy dusts the other two. You can count the number of chairs you have dusted or the number of knobs on the kitchen unit you have wiped. It does require a lot of patience, but at the end of the day it will be less stressful than struggling to do the household chores and dealing with a screaming toddler.

Living far away from close family always presents a problem for parents of young children, and I would suggest that you and your husband have a chat about arranging some other care for your daughter one or two mornings a week. This would allow you time to get the bulk of the chores done, leaving you more time to deal with your daughter on the other days. Check your local library for a list of crèches or nurseries in the area or consider finding a childminder. Do not feel guilty about getting some outside help with your daughter. If you were living nearer your family this would happen automatically without you even thinking that you were sharing the care. It will also help her become less dependent on you and make the arrival of the new baby much easier. If you can't find suitable paid childcare, it might be an idea to team up with another mother and organise regular play dates so that one day you have their child for the afternoon and then the next week she has yours. Finally, do sit down with your husband and discuss and agree ground rules on how you are both going to deal with helping your daughter resolve situations she finds difficult. It is very important that you are both united in how you help her cope and that you are also consistent.

Skills gained during the second year

Walking

While the majority of toddlers are walking soon after their first birthday, it can take several more months of practice to achieve the balance and coordination needed for steady walking. Until this is achieved they do not have the ability to steer themselves properly. During this stage there will be much falling over and bumping into things, which can lead to frustration and tantrums.

Listed below are suggestions and guidelines that will help to make things easier for your toddler during the early stages of walking:

- Toddlers will find it easier to learn to walk if they go barefoot, as splaying their toes enables them to get a better grip. It is also better for muscle tone and the development of the feet. In very cold weather it is preferable for your toddler to wear socks with non-slip soles when he is walking indoors; even the softest shoes can restrict his growth.
- The first toddling steps are often referred to as 'cruising'. A toddler will begin by walking sideways first. He uses both hands to pull himself up and hold onto the furniture and support himself as he moves around. Arrange sturdy furniture closer together to encourage cruising.
- As his balance improves, he begins to use only one hand on the furniture for support. Eventually he becomes confident enough to take a couple of unsupported steps between any small gaps in the furniture.
- As his confidence grows, he relies less and less on the furniture for support, moving further and further away from it. Eventually he takes three or four unsupported steps forward at a time.
- Once he is capable of taking a few steps forward, a push-along toy can help him learn to balance. At first he will be unable to control the speed, so it is important always to supervise him, otherwise he will tend to fall flat as it gets away from him.
- Avoid using the round type of baby walker on wheels. They are responsible for 5,000 accidents a year, and the Chartered Society of Physiotherapists claims they may also hinder physical and mental development.
- Once your toddler has been walking properly for about six weeks, a qualified fitter should measure him for his first pair of shoes. It is important to invest in a pair of shoes that are both the right length and the right width. Shoes that do not support his feet properly could cause permanent damage.

Talking

The sooner a toddler is able to communicate his needs by talking, the easier it becomes for parents to control frustration and tantrums. Children learn to talk by listening, and while it makes sense to spend lots of time talking to your toddler, it is very important that you also give him the opportunity to respond to what you are saying. Communication is a two-way thing and should be fun for your toddler. Although you may not understand much of what he is saying, by showing him you are really interested in his attempts at talking you will encourage him to talk even more. By 15 months most toddlers are able to say between six and eight words, and by 18 months this will have increased to between 20 and 40 words. At two years of age most toddlers are able to string two words together – for example, 'more juice' or 'mummy gone' – and by the time they reach two-and-a-half years most will have a vocabulary of about 200 words. Speech varies greatly from toddler to toddler, but if you have any worries or concerns about your child's speech development it is advisable to seek advice from your health visitor or doctor.

The following guidelines will help encourage your toddler to become a confident talker:

- Reading to your child is an excellent way of increasing his vocabulary, pointing things out as you read the story. Try to spend at least two short quiet spells a day reading to your child, avoiding other distractions such as having the television or radio on or answering the telephone.
- When talking to your toddler, make sure that you speak slowly and clearly and that he is able to see your mouth movements as you pronounce the words. During the second year it is also better to try to keep sentences short and simple. Once your toddler is stringing three and four words together, you can lengthen your sentences.
- Do not correct your toddler when he pronounces a word incorrectly as this will only discourage him; instead it is better to repeat the word back to him correctly. For example, if he says 'bit tat' instead of 'big cat', it is better to reply by saying, 'yes, it's a big black cat' than by forcing him to repeat the word 'cat' correctly.
- All toddlers love to mimic adults, so singing nursery rhymes that involve lots of action and exaggerated facial expression, along with the constant repetition of the same words, is a great way to help your toddler's verbal skills.
- Discuss things as you are doing them with your toddler and emphasise the key words in the sentence. Avoid using pronouns such as 'your' or 'it'. Instead of saying, 'Let's put on

your shoes' or 'Where is it?', I would suggest saying, 'Let's put on James's red shoes' or 'Where's James's blue ball?'

- It is worthwhile making a list of any new words you notice your toddler using and making sure that they are introduced as much as possible into the conversations you and the rest of the family have with him.

- Finally, as your toddler's vocabulary increases, be prepared to repeat yourself over and over again as he constantly asks the same questions. This is all part of your child learning how to talk and the more patient you are when answering his questions, the more eager he will be to communicate.

Q My son of 20 months wants to do everything immediately and gets really angry and upset when it doesn't happen. If I say that Granny is coming this afternoon or we are going to the park later, he whinges on and off until it actually happens. I find that that his whinging and impatient behaviour is leading me to lose my patience, so much so that I sometimes end up shouting at him.

A Toddlers do not start to understand the concept of time until they are nearly three years of age. Therefore I would avoid using expressions such as 'later' or talking about things that are tomorrow or too far ahead. It is better to prepare him for things not too far in advance by bringing the event into context with his daily routine. For example tell him that you will be going to the park after he has had his breakfast, or after his biscuit and juice. Granny is coming to visit after he has had his lunch, and daddy will come home after he has had his tea. While he may still get impatient and keep asking when, explaining this way will help him have a better understanding of when it happens.

Dressing

By the age of 14 months most toddlers have learned how to pull off their hat and their socks. This is an excellent time to introduce activity toys that will help your toddler develop his manipulation skills. Shape sorter toys, and dolls that come with zips, toggles, buttons, etc., will all help him to do this.

It is important to allow extra time once your toddler is learning this skill. He will need lots of encouragement and will quickly sense if you are in a hurry and impatient.

The following guidelines will help your toddler learn to dress and undress himself:

- Between 18 and 24 months, the majority of toddlers will be able to remove most of their clothes, and by 30 months most are capable of getting totally undressed and dressed, but they will still need help with buttons, poppers and braces.
- Your toddler will be less likely to get frustrated or bored if you teach him to undress and dress in stages. Once he is capable of taking off his socks and trousers, move on to him taking off his socks, trousers and pants etc. Use the same approach when teaching him how to dress himself.
- Encourage his independence by allowing him some choice in which clothes he wears, but do limit the choice so that you remain in control.

Q Until recently my daughter of 22 months used to be very co-operative about getting dressed in the morning, and was even managing partially to dress herself. Since spending several days with her doting grandparents, she now simply refuses to get dressed in the morning. She starts running around wanting to play hide and seek or starts playing with her toys or demanding a video.

She goes to a childminder three mornings a week and has to be dropped off by 8.30am so that I can get to my work by 9am. I try to be patient and gently persuade her to co-operate, but with time being so limited I usually end up shouting at her and forcing the clothes on her, which results in us both leaving the house very upset and often in tears.

A It is obvious that your parents had a lot more time to spare in the morning and that dressing became a game that has got out of hand. Using games to get very young toddlers dressed can often work, but it may backfire as the toddler becomes more assertive and uses the games to control the situation in order to get lots of attention. The following plan of attack is one that I have used with many toddlers and young children and should improve the situation within a few days, provided that you are consistent and persistent when she starts her antics. Try to instigate the plan on a day when you do not have the pressure of getting your daughter to nursery and yourself to work.

The previous night you should get your daughter to help you choose and lay out her clothes for the following day.

The following morning, instead of taking her back upstairs straight after breakfast, get her to help you with something like making breadcrumbs for the ducks or packing a cartoon of juice and a biscuit in her rucksack so that you can go to the swings. Talk lots about the impending trip to the park or playground and what fun it is going to be and all the different things and people that will be there. Once you see that you have got her interest, then suggest that she had better get dressed quickly so that you can get to the park. If she starts protesting about getting dressed, say, 'That's fine, we don't have to feed the duck or go to the swings', elaborating on all the exciting things that she is going to miss. This in itself is often enough to get the child upstairs and dressed quickly. If this does happen, you should give her lots of praise and tell her how happy you are that she was such a clever girl getting ready so quickly. When you get to the park you can if you wish buy a very small ice cream or give her a sweet and reinforce that she deserved this very special treat for getting ready quickly like big girls do. It is very important that she sees the treat as a reward for good behaviour that has already happened. Offering her the ice cream as a reward before she has agreed to get dressed will be more like a bribe allowing her to dictate how and when she will do things. If this works, when you get home you should also start a column on a star chart for getting dressed, and put a star on the chart to remind her how good she was at getting dressed. The next few days should follow much the same pattern, with you arranging to take her somewhere of interest so that she is keen to get dressed and gets a star and a small reward when she has done so quickly and without fuss. Once you have established a pattern of her getting dressed without a fuss, you can phase out the small reward to every other day, until you reach a situation where she has to have several stars to get a reward.

If you find that she does not respond to the enticement of

going out on the first day or the strategy fails to work on the second or third day, it is important that you remain calm and ignore her refusal to get dressed. If she starts running around, restrain her gently but firmly for a few minutes so that she is at face level with you, then say simply and firmly, 'If you don't want to get dressed, that's fine, but we don't go anywhere until you are dressed.' Then totally ignore her when she wants your attention. Keep repeating the phrase 'When you're dressed', even if you have to do so 20 times an hour. Do not show any signs of annoyance or anger, and under no circumstances resort to bribing. Make sure that the video and television are turned off at the mains so that she can't get to them, and restrict the toys she can play with until she is dressed. It can often take a couple of hours of following this procedure for two or three days, but if you are consistent and make things as boring as possible for her, she will soon learn that life is more fun when she gets dressed quickly.

When she does start to show willing on getting dressed quickly, give her lots of praise, particularly in front of friends and relatives, for example, 'Sasha was such a clever girl this morning. She got dressed so quickly. Mummy and Daddy were so proud of her,' etc, etc.

It also helps if after breakfast instead of saying, 'Let's get dressed now', you say something like, 'It's going to be so nice to go to the park and play with all your friends. Do you think that Johnny will be there?' or 'I bet those little ducks are very hungry today. Shall we get to the park quickly to feed them?'

Give her lots of suggestions to get her thinking about things that she could be doing. This will encourage her to want to get dressed quickly so that she can go out and enjoy herself, rather than run around the house being totally ignored.

Feeding

A toddler who is still drinking from a bottle and continues to be given lots of puréed and mashed foods during the second year will be much slower at learning to self-feed. To help develop the pincer grip (forefinger and thumb grasp) necessary for confident self-feeding it is essential to introduce lots of finger foods and chopped fruit and vegetables. Feeding bottles should be abandoned by the age of one year, and apart from breast feeds, all drinks should be given from a non-spill type beaker or cup.

The following guidelines will help your toddler learn how to feed himself:

- Between 12 and 15 months most toddlers will attempt to use a spoon, although they will need help with loading it and directing it into their mouth.
- By 18 months a toddler who has had enough practice will manage to eat most of his food by himself using a spoon. Self-feeding with a spoon will be made easier for a toddler if the food is in a bowl.
- At two years of age a toddler should have developed enough hand–eye coordination to eat his food with a small fork and should manage to eat all of his meal without assistance. Toddlers will learn to use cutlery sooner if they are allowed to join in some family meals and encouraged to copy the adults.

Mealtime battles

During the first year, babies grow rapidly. Most babies will have increased their height by 50 per cent and trebled their birth weight by the time they reach their first birthday. In the second year, growth slows down and there is often a very noticeable decrease in the toddler's appetite. Elizabeth Morse says in her book, *My Child Won't Eat*, 'If a child grew at the same rate as in the first year he would be 29 metres [96 feet] long and weigh 200 tonnes by the age of ten'. Unfortunately, many parents are not aware that the decrease in their toddler's appetite is normal. They become anxious that he is not eating enough and often resort to spoon-feeding him in the vain hope that it will get his old appetite back. Unfortunately, the pressure to get the toddler to eat more usually has the opposite effect and results in what many childcare experts term 'food fights'. Mealtimes soon become a battle-ground, with the toddler screaming as his parents insist on him having just one more spoonful. If you wish to avoid these feeding problems with your toddler, or if he is already experiencing them, it is essential that you have a clear understanding of what he needs to eat for a healthy and well-balanced diet. This will help avoid food fights and fussy eating and will also encourage long-term healthy eating habits.

A sample menu for an 18-month-old toddler should look something like this:

Breakfast 7.30–8am
1 cup of full-fat organic milk
50g (2 oz) cereal with milk and chopped fruit
small organic yoghurt
small slice of buttered toast

Mid-Morning 9.30–10am
1 cup of well diluted juice or water
1 small piece of fruit

Lunch 12 noon
50g (2 oz) of chicken or white fish
2 small broccoli or cauliflower florets
1 chopped carrot or 1 baby corn
1 tablespoon of peas
1 cup of well diluted juice or water

Mid-Afternoon 3pm
1 cup of well diluted juice or water
1 small piece of fruit, rice cake or plain cookie

Tea 5pm
Pasta with a tablespoon of mixed vegetables and sauce
1 small chopped apple with yoghurt or cheese
1 small cup of milk, well diluted juice or water

Bedtime 7–7.30pm
1 cup of full-fat organic milk

Very important: Fruit juice should always be well diluted and ideally given only at mealtimes as this reduces the possibility of damage to your toddler's teeth. Try to restrict juice to no more than two cups per day.

For further details of what kinds of foods to offer your child please refer to Chapter 5 of this book and find the section that discusses your child's age group.

Food refusal

It is vital that mealtimes do not become a battle of wills. How you deal with any feeding problems at this stage may affect your toddler's attitude to food for the rest of his life. In my experience, toddlers who are going through a fussy stage and who are constantly coaxed, bribed or force-fed by spoon, nearly always end up with a long-term eating problem.

If you are concerned that your toddler may not be eating enough, it is a good idea to keep a food diary for one week. Each day list all the food and drink he has taken, as well as the times of consumption. Because a toddler's appetite can vary considerably from day to day, it is important that you calculate his overall food intake over one week. Most parents find that over several days the amount of food their toddler has eaten averages out to meet all his nutritional requirements. However, if your toddler's food diary shows that he is actually eating less than the recommended amounts, it would be advisable to discuss things with your doctor or health visitor.

Below are listed the most common causes of food refusal and faddiness, together with some guidelines to encourage good eating habits and help avoid long-term problems:

- Drinking excessive amounts of milk is a major cause of toddlers refusing to eat. They need a minimum of 350ml (12oz) and a maximum of 600ml (20oz) per day (inclusive of milk used in food). The bottle should be abandoned at one year, and after that all milk drinks should be given in a beaker or a cup.
- Fruit juice given immediately before food or within an hour prior to eating can take the edge off a toddler's appetite. Encourage your toddler to eat half of his food before giving him the drink. If possible, try to get your toddler used to drinking water in between meals. If juice is given, make sure it is very well diluted, and offer it no later than two hours before his mealtime.
- Many leading brands of fromage frais are high in sugar, containing sometimes as much as 14.5g (0.5oz) in a 100g (4oz) pot. Sugar is often the second largest ingredient in the pot. Toddlers can become addicted to these and, if given them often enough, will soon lose their appetite for other foods.

- Try to offer a variety of different foods in small amounts, rather than one or two in large amounts. For example, serving fish with a small amount of carrots, cauliflower, peas and potatoes is more likely to stimulate the toddler's taste buds than serving fish with carrots and potatoes. By offering him a selection of the foods you know he likes, you will be encouraging him at least to try some of them.
- It is best to serve your toddler's main protein meal at lunchtime, and then if he becomes fussy and tired later in the day, you know he has had one good meal and you can be more relaxed about tea. He can then be offered something quick and easy such as pasta or a baked potato with a filling, or a thick soup and sandwiches.
- Schedule meals and snacks at regular times and stick to these times. If after 30 minutes your toddler is not showing any interest in eating, remove the food without making any comment on his lack of appetite. However, he should not be allowed anything to eat or drink until the next scheduled meal or snack. Ideally, there should be a two-hour gap between meals and snacks.
- Eating even the smallest of snacks less than two hours before a meal can be enough to affect some toddlers' appetites. The type of snack given is significant. Foods that take longer to digest will be more likely to take the edge off your toddler's appetite.
- Avoid giving your toddler puddings or sweets as an incentive for finishing his meal. This only leads him to think that the food can't be that good if you are offering him a bribe to eat it. Instead, offer a selection of fresh fruit, cheese and crackers, or plain yoghurt mixed with fresh mashed fruit.
- Try to avoid distractions at mealtimes such as reading or playing games. Also remember that every time you speak to your toddler he will need to answer. Therefore be careful about getting into long-winded conversations before he has managed to eat most of his meal.

Encouraging good eating habits

Mealtimes should be happy and relaxed occasions. It is unfair to expect a child under two years old to eat without some degree of mess. At this stage, as long as a toddler is eating well and enjoying his food, no comment should be made about any mess that he may make. However, if he starts playing with his food and throwing it on the floor, it is best to assume that he is not hungry and remove his plate.

Forcing a toddler to eat when he is not really hungry will only create a more serious problem. This can be avoided if you ensure that your toddler's daily intake of food and drink is properly structured. A toddler who becomes overtired, or over-hungry, will behave in the same way as the overtired or over-hungry baby – he will not eat well. Therefore it is important to be consistent with the timing of meals. In my experience, breakfast should be finished by 8 am so that the toddler is ready to eat a good lunch at around 12 noon and tea at no later than 5pm. Snacks should only be given midway between meals, as even the smallest amount of food or drink can take the edge off a toddler's appetite. A toddler who is having breakfast at around 7.30am should be offered a mid-morning snack and drink between 9.30am and 10am, and a mid-afternoon snack and drink no later then 3pm.

Behaviour

Walking, talking, dressing and feeding are the main skills that a toddler has to learn during his second year. However, there are many other daily hurdles that he will face, and it is inevitable that there will be times when he gets so frustrated that he feels unable to cope. Just as an electrical circuit will blow a fuse when the system is overloaded, the toddler whose emotions become overloaded with frustration and anger will also blow a fuse; this is referred to as a tantrum. Tantrums are a normal part of a child's development; they are his way of communicating to his parents that he can't manage.

Tantrums

Around a toddler's first birthday difficult behaviour and more often than not tantrums begin to appear. This coincides with the time most children begin to walk. Tantrums reach a peak around the second birthday (hence the phrase 'terrible twos'), and by the third birthday they are on the decline. A child having a full-blown tantrum will shout and scream hysterically, and throw himself around the room or on the floor, kicking out at anything he can.

Severe tantrums like this are very stressful for both the child and the parents, and action should be taken to prevent this sort of tantrum becoming a regular occurrence.

During this critical stage of your toddler's development in which he has so many new skills to master, he is likely to get very frustrated. Therefore it is essential that social activities and sleep be carefully structured so that he doesn't become overtired. In my experience, toddlers and children who are allowed to become overtired are much more prone to having full-blown temper tantrums, than those whose activities and sleep are carefully structured. Prevention is better than cure, and an understanding on your part of the causes of tantrums will go a long way towards helping your toddler to avoid them.

Listed below are the main causes of frustration that can lead to temper tantrums:

- The toddler has the mental capacity to understand virtually everything that is said to him but does not yet have the verbal skills necessary to communicate how he feels or what he really wants.
- His desire to become more independent will lead him to attempt physical tasks beyond his capabilities.
- A toddler will eat exactly the amount he needs to satisfy his hunger. Being forced to eat just one more spoonful to satisfy the parent's perception of what he needs is sure to lead to a tantrum.
- A child who has too many new toys, watches too many videos or attends too many activity classes, will cease to use his imagination and quickly become bored if he is not entertained the whole time. Boredom quickly turns into frustration if his demands to be entertained are not met immediately.
- Lengthy shopping trips with toddlers nearly always end in tears. If possible, arrange for a friend with a toddler to watch both of them for a couple of hours while you do your big shop. This can be reciprocated later.
- Think twice before using the word 'no'. Overuse of the word can result in it not having the desired effect when you really do mean it.
- Both parents should work by the same set of rules; otherwise the toddler will become confused as to what is acceptable behaviour and what is not.

Dealing with tantrums

Being aware of the main causes that lead to toddler tantrums can help a parent to see a tantrum brewing and step in before the matter gets out of hand – and before it becomes a serious habit. However, when feelings of anger, jealousy, fear and frustration get too much, there is bound to be a tantrum, as this is the way in which your toddler will express the inner turmoil that he is feeling. He is neither trying to annoy you nor being deliberately naughty and should not be punished. How to deal with the situation depends very much on his age and the reason for the tantrum, but it is important that he is neither punished nor rewarded.

Listed below are guidelines that will help you deal with your toddler's tantrums.

- Diversion: The majority of parents I know believe that diversion is one of the best methods of dealing with a tantrum. In order for distraction to be effective you must get his attention at the beginning of the tantrum, before he has worked himself up into a frenzy. The following three distractions are the ones that I have found to be the most effective.

a) The majority of toddlers love playing with water so get your toddler to wash the baby's bottles or some plastic containers. If it is close to a mealtime, get him to help you wash some of the vegetables and fruit. On a warm day suggest that he helps you water the garden.

b) Keep a small selection of balloons, party hats and poppers at hand and bring them out when you see he is about to throw a wobbly. Alternatively, give him a small bubble-blowing kit to play with; they can keep some children happy for ages.

c) Some parents keep a slab of ready-made pastry in the fridge and suggest a spot of baking when they notice their toddler is about to lose it. All the pounding and squeezing of the dough soon gets rid of excess frustration.

- Time out: Time out is the next most popular method used by parents when distraction fails and a child is having a full-blown temper tantrum. Placing him in his cot with the door shut for a short period of time is a particularly effective way of dealing with a toddler who decides to throw a tantrum in front of grandparents, relatives or friends, whose well-meaning interventions usually make matters worse.

• Holding time: A small number of parents say that holding their toddler closely and firmly and talking to him in a soothing tone of voice until he calms down sometimes works. In my experience this can work only if he has not already worked himself up into a rage, if he is small and easy to grab hold of, or is sensitive and not very strong-willed.

• Withdrawing attention: Some parents believe that the best way to deal with their toddler's tantrum is to let it run its course and totally ignore it. If necessary, go to another room so that the child realises he is no longer the centre of attention. I have occasionally seen this approach work but it has always been in families who are fortunate enough to have child-safe playrooms in full view of the kitchen. It may be worthwhile trying to ignore your child, but it is important that he is not left in a situation where he could harm himself.

Aggressive behaviour
The majority of toddlers will occasionally use some form of aggressive behaviour, such as hitting, kicking, biting or scratching. In my experience, toddlers who resort to this sort of aggressive behaviour usually do so when they are feeling insecure. Some feel resentful and jealous when they suddenly find they have to share their parents' attention with a new baby, or share the toys with other children at playgroup. A toddler who has not yet learned to share may try to retrieve his toy from another by kicking. The mother breast-feeding the new baby may be subjected to a sudden bite from a toddler who is feeling neglected. A gentle stroke of the baby's cheek by the toddler may end up as a very severe scratch. Although all of these spur-of-the-moment attacks are intentional, they are not planned and the toddler does not yet understand what causes him to make them. Unlike tantrums, which are usually directed only at the parents, aggressive behaviour can often be directed at anyone whom the toddler feels is a threat. The toddler who gets into the habit of using aggressive behaviour as a way of asserting himself or of getting undivided attention will quickly become very unpopular with other parents and children.

If you think your toddler's aggressive behaviour is a result of sibling rivalry please refer to Chapter 6 for further advice.

The following guidelines give suggestions on how to deal with a toddler's aggressive behaviour:

- A toddler must learn that aggressive behaviour in any form is not acceptable. Therefore it is foolish to deal with this problem by smacking him or, even worse, as some books suggest, 'biting him back'.
- If your toddler lashes out aggressively in one way or another, immediately take him to one side and explain simply and firmly that biting, hitting, etc. is not allowed. Avoid using words like 'bad' or 'naughty', which will only make him feel more insecure.
- Reinforce his good behaviour with lots of encouragement and praise, with much emphasis on the times he plays nicely with the baby and other toddlers.
- Be extra vigilant when he is in group situations and quickly divert his attention when he shows signs of frustration and irritability.
- A toddler should never be left alone with a baby for even a few minutes, and when they are together, they should be kept in full view.

The following case study describes a scenario that I have witnessed many times over the years. It describes how a temper tantrum can result in aggressive behaviour.

Isabella, aged 18 months

Isabella was very much a contented little baby for the first year of her life. She was a good eater and sleeper, with a sunny nature and ready smile. She had two older sisters of four and six and was the much loved baby of the family. For her first year-and-a-half she was the easiest and most loving child, adored by her big sisters and her parents.

At about 18 months Isabella began to hit her sisters. She was a very happy little girl but tended to resort to smacking her sisters if she wanted their attention. Both elder girls were naturally gentle and never once retaliated. Soon after this, Isabella began to hit her parents. Isabella's mother would pick Isabella up for a cuddle or a kiss, and Isabella would use both hands to smack her mother's cheeks, as if she was clapping. Her mother had never had to deal with this sort of problem before. She was baffled, since her older daughters had never demonstrated this behaviour, and when she had seen other children being physically unpleasant she had always thought the parents were responsible for not being firmer.

Isabella's mother had never smacked Isabella or her sisters, although when her elder daughters were toddlers she did sit them on a 'naughty stair' on the rare occasions when they were repeatedly naughty. She was soon to discover that the 'naughty stair' had no effect on Isabella, and her toddler found this 'punishment' such fun that she would often hit her sisters and then run to the naughty stair as if it was a game.

Isabella's mother sought my advice when Isabella began to hit other children. She recognised that the first couple of times when Isabella had smacked her sisters, the family had been mildly amused by their baby's feisty character. She also recognised that since Isabella was the youngest and much adored baby of the family, they had all been rather more indulgent to and tolerant of her exuberant behaviour than was sensible. While Isabella's mother recognised that this behaviour was not uncommon in toddlers, she was concerned that the more she tried to prevent Isabella hitting, the more amused her child seemed to be. Her mother also felt it was very unfair on her elder daughters that they had to put up with this when they were so kind and patient to their little sister. We discussed the fact that Isabella adored being the centre of attention and that as a bright child she had discovered that hitting was an immediate way to have everyone's attention. I commended Isabella's mother for not resorting to smacking, since we both felt that it is inappropriate to smack a child when the lesson you are trying to teach is that it was wrong to hit.

The first advice I gave to Isabella's mother was that the next time Isabella hit her or her sisters, all the family should firmly say 'No, Isabella' and then to avoid eye contact. It was important to be very clear that this was not a game and that her naughty behaviour would not be rewarded with attention. Secondly, I encouraged Isabella's mother to defuse situations where Isabella *was able to hit her sisters. If her sister was lying on the floor when Isabella hit her, I suggested she immediately tell her elder daughter to put herself out of reach – sitting up in a chair or going to her bedroom. Similarly, if Isabella hit her mother during a cuddle, her mother was to put her down and immediately turn her attention to something else.*

Within a week, the family's new response to Isabella's hitting was having a good effect. Isabella still occasionally hit her family, but having discovered it didn't produce a very interesting response, her hitting become less common and more half-hearted.

Finally, I encouraged her mother to tell Isabella that she would have to go to her cot if she repeated her behaviour. Isabella's mother was concerned this would effect Isabella's happiness in her cot, since she had always been very good about going to bed, and loved lying and playing in her bed. However, I reassured her that it was very unlikely that she would need to put Isabella in her cot more than once or twice, so there was little chance that this would affect her good sleep associations with it.

On the next occasion when Isabella hit her sister, Isabella's mother gathered her up and carried her to her cot, where she was left for a couple of minutes. Isabella was astonished and upset. She understood that this was the result of hitting her sister, She began to cry and shout 'orry' – her word for 'sorry'. Her mother gave her a big cuddle and asked her to give her big sister a kiss.

Isabella is now nearly two and has not hit anyone in her family or social circle for more than two months. She is a delightful, loving little girl whose behaviour is no longer marred by episodes of hitting her sisters, parents or friends.

Problems with praise

Parents use praise to show their children they approve of things they consider to be well done. The problem with this is that the praise is based solely on the parents' judgement and evaluation of the child's behaviour. It leaves no room for the child's point of view. Jane Nelson, psychologist and mother of seven children, believes that the overuse of praise to improve behaviour can result in children becoming pleasers and approval 'junkies'. In her book *Positive Discipline* she explains how these children (and later adults) develop self-concepts that are totally dependent on the opinions of others. Other children, she claims, can resent and rebel against praise, either because they don't want to live up to the expectations of others or because they fear they can't compete with those who seem to get praise so easily. The long-term effect of praise is often that a child becomes too dependent on others.

Nelson believes that encouragement is preferable to praise, as it takes into consideration the child's point of view, inspiring self-evaluation that will lead to the child becoming more self- confident and independent. While I still think praise is an important tool of parenthood, it should be used with caution. Since reading this excellent book I have come to agree with the author that encouragement, along with praising the actual deed rather than the child himself, is the most effective way to improve behaviour.

To try to understand how a child may perceive praise, think of how we as adults feel when we receive it. For example we can probably all remember a time when we spent hours preparing for a special dinner party for a partner or close friend – the amount of hard work it took to shop, prepare and cook the perfect meal and then present the meal and yourself to the best of your ability. As the guests bid their farewells and thanked you for the splendid evening, which of the following comments from your partner or friend would mean more to you?

Example one: 'You're such a star. I am so lucky to have such a great wife/husband/partner/friend; I don't know what I would do without you. You looked beautiful and, as always, got everything right. I am so proud of you.'

Example two: 'Thank you for making the evening such a success. I really appreciate all the time and effort you put into cooking such a fantastic meal. I think everyone enjoyed the evening. How about you? Did you enjoy yourself?'

Example one is all based on the partner/friend's perception of what he or she expects from you and how you should look, act and behave. On receiving the compliment, it is hardly likely that you would think: Yes I am a star and very beautiful, and you're very lucky to have me, as I am always capable of getting everything right. You would probably feel patronised and under a great deal of pressure to live up to expectations.

Example two takes into consideration not only the hard work that you have put into the dinner party, but also the partner/friend's concern about whether you also enjoyed yourself. Example two is based on appreciation, respect and empathy, unlike example one, which is based on direct praise of personality.

Sleeping problems

Waking in the night
Even the most contented little baby who has always slept well during his first year can suddenly develop sleep problems during the second. There are several reasons why a toddler who as a baby always settled well at bedtime and slept through the night, suddenly refuses to go to sleep or wakes several times a night.

Listed below are the most common causes that I have found for a toddler waking in the night, together with some suggestions for dealing with these wakings:

Routine
During the second year toddlers become more mobile and usually begin to attend more activities. This can leave them physically and mentally exhausted. Those who do not have a regular daytime nap or a specific bedtime are more prone to overtiredness, which itself can result in night-time wakings. It is essential to establish a regular time for the daytime nap and for bedtime and then to stick to it.

Too much sleep
It is very easy to miss the signs that a child is ready to cut back on the amount of sleep he needs during the day. This can result in night-time problems. At one year most babies are still having an average of 14–15 hours of sleep a day, divided between night-time sleep and two daytime naps. However, as a baby enters toddlerhood the amount of sleep he needs is reduced to an average of 13–14 hours a day, which is usually divided between night-time sleep and one daytime nap. Watching for the signs that your toddler is ready to cut back on his sleep can help avoid night-time sleep problems evolving.

The following are indications that your toddler is probably ready to cut down on his hours of daily sleep:

- He is between the ages of 15 and 18 months. At this stage the majority of toddlers will show signs of needing to cut back their sleep.
- He takes longer and longer to drop off to sleep when put down for his nap at 9.30am or may settle well but cut the amount of time he sleeps down to 15–20 minutes.
- He sleeps well at the morning nap but cuts right back on his lunchtime nap.
- He takes longer to settle and sleep in the evening or begins to wake up earlier in the morning.

By watching for the above signs you will be able to structure your toddler's daytime sleep to ensure that his night-time sleep is not affected.

Dummy

A toddler who has been allowed to have a dummy in bed can wake up several times a night if he loses the dummy. The only way to deal with this problem is to get rid of the dummy altogether. Please refer to Chapter 7.

New baby

The arrival of a new baby can sometimes cause a toddler to wake in the night. Try to structure your routine so that you manage to give your toddler some undivided attention during the day. When you attend to him in the night keep the reassurances short and simple and do not get involved in long discussions. A toddler who is feeling neglected during the day will try to make up in the night for the attention that he feels he is missing. For further information please refer to Chapter 6.

Anxiety

The arrival of a new baby, a house move, starting nursery or separation anxiety when a mother returns to work can cause a toddler to be anxious and start waking in the night. Sometimes buying a special cuddly toy that stays in the cot at all times can help make the toddler feel more secure. Special attention should be given to the toddler during the day to help overcome his feelings of anxiety. If your child is attending a nursery or another form of childcare, I suggest that you make time to discuss the situation with the carer, asking them to be particularly sensitive towards your child's feelings during this time. When you get back from work make sure that you spend extra time talking and listening to your child. If you have more than one child, I would suggest asking your partner or a grandparent to occupy the others while you spend a little time alone with your toddler once or twice a week.

Stories and videos

During the latter part of the second year a toddler's imagination becomes more active, and choosing the wrong bedtime stories or videos can over-stimulate or upset some toddlers. Try to avoid excessive video watching prior to bedtime and choose simple stories that do not stimulate or frighten.

Tantrums

Tears before bedtime can often result in the toddler waking in the night. Tantrums that end in tears are usually caused by over-excitement, over-stimulation or confrontation. It is essential that bedtime rituals are kept calm and consistent.

The big bed

In my experience, transferring your toddler to a big bed before he is ready can be a major cause of night-time waking. Many parents make this transfer between 18 months and two years of age, often prompted by the fact a new baby is on the way and the cot will be needed. Other parents listen to the advice of friends who say that their toddler sleeps much better now he is in a bed. To me this implies that their toddler's sleeping habits were probably not very good in the first place!

The majority of my clients leave their toddlers in a cot until they are nearly three years of age. Because all of these toddlers are still sleeping in a sleeping bag, the possibility of them trying to climb out of the cot never arises. If a cot is needed for a second baby, many parents choose to buy a second cot, or a cot bed into which the toddler can be transferred before the new baby arrives. This can eventually be used as a first bed for the second baby.

Before transferring your toddler to a bed consider the following points:

- A toddler who is transferred to a bed too soon is more likely to wake up early or get up in the night. He is inclined to get more upset than an older child when parents try to settle him back to sleep in his own bed, and often ends up sleeping in his parents' bed.
- The arrival of a new baby often prompts the toddler to get out of bed if he hears the baby crying in the night. He quickly learns to demand the same attention as the baby in the night – feeds and a cuddle.
- A toddler who is sleeping in a bed will be more likely to take his nappy off in the night, even if he is not able to get through the night without a nappy.
- Once a nappy is no longer needed at night, a potty and a night light usually have to be put in the toddler's room. In my experience, toddlers under three years of age who are sleeping in a bed and who need to have a night light are much more likely to wake in the night and be difficult to settle back to sleep.

Sarah, aged 23 months

Sarah had never slept well as a baby. Indeed, she did not sleep properly through the night until she was sleep trained at 18 months. After 18 months of waking up two and three times a night, her mother was delighted to settle for Sarah going to bed around 9pm and waking at 6–7am. Sarah also took a nap of two hours in the middle of the day, which helped her mother cope with her difficult behaviour between 6.30pm and 9pm, after which she would fall asleep exhausted in the cot, drinking her bottle of formula. This pattern continued until her brother was born five months later.

Simon weighed over 10lb (4.5kg) at birth and by four weeks had outgrown the small Moses basket he had been sleeping in. Because Sarah had occasionally slept in a bed at her grandmother's house, the obvious decision was to put Sarah in the big bed and give Simon the cot.

The first night Sarah was so excited about going into her big bed that it took her mother slightly longer than usual to settle her to sleep. Sarah would keep getting in and out of the bed, demanding yet another story to be read. She eventually fell asleep in her mother's arms at around 9.40pm, only to wake screaming at around midnight. Sarah's mother had to spend another hour lying on the bed with her before she fell asleep. She awoke twice more in the night and each time it took nearly an hour to settle her. The following evening Sarah took even longer to settle, falling asleep at 10.15pm. As on the previous night, she woke up three times. During the following week a pattern quickly emerged of Sarah not settling to sleep until nearly 11pm and waking two or three times in the night. She would only fall asleep if her mother read or sang to her, which could take anything up to two hours.

When her mother rang me for help it was clear that putting Sarah in the big bed was a major contribution to Sarah's sleeping problems. I suggested that she should put Sarah back in her cot. Fortunately, a friend had a spare cot that could be borrowed for Simon, and Sarah was transferred back to her old cot. The number of night wakings was immediately reduced, and when she did wake, her mother managed to settle her back to sleep quickly. However, settling Sarah at bedtime continued to be a problem. Her mother would start settling her at 9pm but she did not usually fall asleep until between 10pm and 11pm. I believe that the reason for this was that, like a baby who associates falling asleep with being fed or rocked, Sarah associated falling asleep with being read or sung to.

When Sarah was transferred to the bed and resisted sleep, the already late bedtime meant she got very overtired and fought sleep even more. Therefore the time her mother spent reading and singing began to get longer and longer. I advised her mother gradually to bring Sarah's bedtime forward by 30 minutes every three nights until it was 7.30pm and spend no more than 20 minutes singing and reading to Sarah. Because Sarah had been used to a late bedtime for so long, I suggested that her mother should play a tape of gentle nursery rhymes for 40 minutes after leaving the room. She should tell Sarah that she was going to have a bath and would come back for one final 'night-night' when the tape was finished. If Sarah shouted out, she was to say that she was in the bath and would come soon. By the time the tape was finished Sarah was always fast asleep. Within two weeks the length of time the tape was played was reduced to 20 minutes, and Sarah was sleeping from 7.30pm to 7am. Each morning Sarah's mother would tell her that she had gone in after the bath and given her a big night-night kiss.

Daytime naps

During the second year, it becomes easier to adapt the original routine and parents can get into the habit of being relaxed about timing. Structuring your toddler's sleep is still very important if you wish to avoid him becoming overtired, which in turn can lead to sleep problems.

The morning nap

If your baby has been following the CLB routines during his first year and sleeps well between 7pm and 7am between the age of 12 and 18 months he will normally start to cut back on the early morning nap. He will either take longer and longer to drop off to sleep when he is put down for his nap at 9–9.30pm or continue to go straight off to sleep but wake up after 10–15 minutes. When he reaches the stage where it is such a short nap many parents allow this nap to be taken in the buggy on the way to the park, shops or playgroup. If your toddler is nearer 18 months and only sleeping 10–15 minutes, he can probably manage to get through happily to lunchtime nap without this nap, and you could try dropping it altogether. If he is just over a year he would probably not manage to get through without this short nap, so it would be advisable to keep it slightly longer.

Another sign that a toddler is ready to cut out the morning nap is that the lunchtime sleep is getting shorter. Some toddlers will show no signs of reducing the amount of time they sleep in the morning and will cut back on the lunchtime nap. This suits some mothers as it allows them to get many more chores done in the morning without a toddler in tow. The problem with allowing a longer nap in the morning is that once the toddler is only having one nap a day, he will be awake right through from 12 noon to 7pm. Some toddlers eventually get so exhausted by the evening that they fall straight into a very deep sleep the minute they are in bed. This usually has the knock-on effect of the toddler waking earlier in the morning. The earlier waking means that he will become very tired earlier and that the nap comes even earlier. A vicious circle soon emerges where the toddler is starting his day at 6am or earlier.

If at 18 months your toddler is sleeping well at night and lunch-time and still sleeping between 30 and 40 minutes in the morning, I would advise gradually reducing the morning nap over a few weeks until he is only having 10 to 15 minutes anyway, avoiding the opportunity of a problem arising at his other sleep times. Once he is getting through to his lunchtime happily on 10–15 minutes it can be cut out altogether.

Some toddlers do have difficulty making the transition from two naps to one nap and will get slightly more irritable until their body clock has adjusted. In my opinion it is better to put up with a couple of weeks of grumpiness while you establish one good nap of two hours than to end up with two naps of only 45 minutes each and a toddler who is irritable all afternoon because he has become overtired from too short a lunchtime nap.

The early waker

If your toddler appears to need only 11 hours' sleep at night instead of 12 hours and is waking much earlier than 7am, he will probably still need to go down for his nap around 9am. In my experience toddlers who wake early and go down early for the morning nap usually need to go down earlier for the lunchtime nap. As toddlers are much more active physically during the second year they are more prone to becoming very exhausted in the late afternoon and often need to go to bed earlier than 7pm. This only reinforces the early morning waking. I would advise that regardless of how early your toddler wakes you gradually push the morning nap forward by five minutes every three to four days, so that his lunchtime nap eventually becomes later. This should have the knock-on effect of him not being so tired in the late afternoon, which means you could gradually delay his bedtime by five minutes every three to four nights. This will hopefully result in him waking up later in the morning. If he does start to wake up later in the morning, it is very important that you begin to reduce the amount of time he sleeps in the morning to 10–15 minutes, so that his overall daily sleep is no more than 13½ hours, slightly less than the average amount of sleep needed by a toddler.

Bedtime battles

Very often bedtime can change from being a peaceful and easy time to a fraught and exhausting one. The situation can quickly deteriorate into a battle of wills, and it is very important to tackle the problem before bad habits are formed. I believe that the main cause for these bedtime battles is an overtired and over-stimulated child.

The following points should help you to minimise bedtime battles:

- Try to ensure that your toddler has his main protein meal of the day at lunchtime. This means that tea can be something quick and easy to prepare, such as pasta or a thick soup with sandwiches.
- Between the ages of one and two your toddler still needs at least one-and-a-half hours of daytime sleep.
- During the afternoon do not allow your toddler to keep taking different toys out of the cupboard if he has not tidied away the ones he has finished with. Encourage him to tidy away all or at least some of his toys.
- Tea should be ready and your toddler seated at 5pm sharp, and he should be taken into the bathroom no later than 5.45pm, to allow plenty of time for the bath and for winding down.

Q My son aged 16 months used to love being read to at bedtime. He would sit happily for up to half an hour, but now he will barely sit still for more than five to ten minutes. His concentration span seems to be decreasing the older he gets. He is becoming more and more boisterous after his bath, running around shouting loudly and throwing his toys all over the place. The more I try to calm him down and get him interested in his books, the worse he becomes, and his usual bedtime of 7.30pm is now nearer 8.30pm.

A Toddlers of this age have an enormous amount of physical energy and very little mental concentration. Getting the right balance of physical and mental activities during the day is critical if bedtime battles are to be avoided. Ensure that your toddler is getting enough physical exercise and fresh air during the earlier part of the day so that he does not build up excess energy for the evening. Encouraging him to walk upstairs, undress himself and put his dirty clothes in the laundry basket will not only teach him vital skills but will also tire him out.

In my experience it is also better at this age to limit story-telling at bedtime to no more than 10–15 minutes, as toddlers are very prone to getting a second wind if the bedtime routine is too long. It is also important to remove any possible distractions that interfere with his concentration.

A bedroom full of accessible toys is often the cause of toddlers becoming distracted at bedtime. Try to limit the number of toys in his bedroom and most certainly remove any that could encourage boisterous behaviour to another room. At this age it is important to choose simple books and to involve him in the story reading by getting him to turn the pages and point the different characters out, encouraging him to repeat any simple words.

You should also examine closely the amount of time he is sleeping during the day. If he is still having two naps, it may be that he is ready to cut one of them out. Sleeping later than 2.30pm can also cause problems at bedtime, and it may be worth rescheduling his daytime sleep, so that he is awake by 2.30pm.

Late bedtime

Some toddlers who have been used to a much later bedtime and settled well may suddenly begin to play up between the ages of 18 months and two years, usually when their daytime sleep is reduced to one nap, and they are attending more activities during the day. The toddler becomes so overtired that he ends up fighting sleep for hours. The already late bedtime of 8.30 or 9pm suddenly ends up being 11pm or later. If this is happening with your toddler, it is essential to bring the bedtime forward to avoid him becoming overtired. Provided that overtiredness is the only problem, it should be possible to get your toddler to go to bed earlier without resorting to 'controlled crying'.

The following guidelines give suggestions for bringing the bedtime forward and avoiding overtiredness, which results in the toddler being more difficult to settle:

- Try to ensure that your toddler gets plenty of fresh air and exercise during the day. This will help to make him more tired so that he needs to sleep earlier.
- Avoid noisy games and excitement after tea, as well as during and after the bath.
- Do not let your toddler watch a video before the bath. A video after the bath can be used as an incentive to get ready for bed.
- Whatever time your toddler is used to going to bed, bring it forward by 30 minutes to allow enough time to establish the ritual of a drink, a story or a video after the bath and teeth cleaning before bed. Remember to dim the lights after the bath.
- Allow three nights to establish the above bedtime ritual and then gradually bring the bedtime forward by 10 minutes every three nights.
- Once the bedtime has been brought forward to 7.30pm, continue to be consistent with the ritual after the bath. Never increase it by more than 30 minutes, as this allows the toddler to get a 'second wind'.
- A toddler who is not quite ready to sleep after the ritual can be allowed to listen to a nursery rhyme or story tape. This can be a great help in teaching him how to get off to sleep by himself.
- It is important to ensure your toddler gets into bed when he is awake, because just as feeding or rocking a baby to sleep can cause problems, so can reading or cuddling a toddler to sleep.

If despite following all the above guidelines, your toddler continues to fight sleep at 7–7.30pm, then you may have to incorporate the crying down or controlled crying methods as described in my book, *The Complete Sleep Guide for Contented Babies and Toddlers,* also published by Vermilion.

2

The Third Year
(24 to 36 months)

By the time a toddler reaches his second birthday his walking will be much steadier and he will become more daring physically as he attempts to run, climb and jump. He will also become less frustrated mentally, because he is able to communicate his needs better as he begins to string words together. However, during the third year he will be faced with a whole host of new challenges. Helping to build his self-esteem will give him the confidence to deal with them. They will include forming friendships with other children and learning how to share; starting nursery school and taking instruction in a group situation; learning good manners and respect for others; taking more responsibility for his own actions and learning about bladder and bowel control by potty training. During this stage of development it is important that parents teach their child how to think and do not think for him.

Self-esteem and confidence

While it is important to teach a child to be cautious of certain things (i.e. the busy road, the steep stairs, etc.), parents should be careful not to protect their child so much that he loses his natural instinct to explore and the courage to try new things.

We have all watched children in the playground as they line up to climb the steps of the slide; one by one they slide down, squealing with delight as they do so. But in nearly every line-up there is the nervous child who climbs the steps extra carefully and very slowly, repeatedly looking back for a nod of reassurance from an anxious parent.

A child who is constantly reminded to be careful when he

attempts everyday challenges, will quickly lose the confidence and the courage to try different things and learn new skills.

Parents who correct everything their child says or does can often damage their child's self-esteem. The desire for their child to achieve success in everything he attempts to do leads some parents to re-arrange the farmyard properly, finish off the edges of the colouring correctly, and more often than not answer for the child when he is asked a question or finish sentences for him. The drive for perfection can very quickly cripple a child's natural ability to try things for himself. He then becomes too anxious to try anything for fear of getting it wrong – frightened of disapproval.

The following are suggestions for helping to build your child's self-esteem and confidence:

• The way a parent helps their child approach the many challenges he faces has a great influence on how successful he will be in mastering the challenge. All too often I hear parents express concern that their child is bound to be like them and be frightened of heights, have no sense of balance, dislike dogs, etc. Every child is unique and it is important not to assume that your child's strengths and weaknesses will be the same as your own.

• Between two and three years of age a child is becoming aware of being a separate person and is beginning to form views and opinions of others. It is very important that you allow your child time to think and answer for himself when he is asked a question.

• During the third year all children are capable of self-feeding, undressing and, apart from buttons and zips, dressing themselves. Continuing to do these things for your child because it is quicker will do little to help his growing independence. Allow extra time at mealtimes and in the morning and evening so you have the patience to guide him and encourage him to do these things for himself.

• When teaching new skills it is important that you choose a time when your child is not overtired or hungry. Then, before doing it together, show him several times how it is done. Once he attempts it by himself it is important to praise him for his efforts even if he doesn't get it quite right.

- Second children appear to learn many skills much more quickly, probably because they copy their elder brother or sister. An only child will benefit greatly from being given the opportunity to mix with other children at playgroups or on play dates.
- It is important not to undermine your child's attempts at something new by comparing him with others. The length of time a child takes to learn a new skill varies from child to child. The important thing is that your child enjoys learning the new skill, not how long he takes to learn it. If you are concerned about your child's development, it is better to talk to your health visitor than to worry unnecessarily.
- Learning a new skill requires a lot of concentration from a child, which can sometimes lead to frustration and anger. If, despite being shown several times, your child is still struggling with a new task or a difficult jigsaw or game, try to resist interfering or doing it for him. It is much better to defuse the situation by suggesting a rest period with a drink and a biscuit. Once he has calmed down and is relaxed he will be much more likely to listen to your advice on how to tackle the task.

During the third year most parents work hard to help build their child's self-esteem and to encourage him to become more confident. However, sometimes a child's increasing independence can cause him to become overconfident, which can lead to disobedience. I think it is essential that parents strike a happy balance between encouraging their child's newfound confidence and teaching them that there are certain rules to which we must all adhere.

Dealing with common fears

During the second year, a child becomes much more aware of the world around him and can be disconcerted to discover that he is not always at the very centre of situations. This in turn can lead to more complex behaviour as he tries to make sense of new experiences, ones that he does not always understand. Children learn very much by example and are acutely sensitive to their parents' reaction to events. In the same way, children learn so much by example that Mummy's frightened response to a cat or dog or Daddy's dislike of the dentist or fear of heights can easily teach a child to be frightened of the same things. I have also noticed that parents who reprimand their children in an aggressive manner or harsh tone of voice can often instil a sense of fear in them. They often become anxious or nervous about trying new things for fear of getting them wrong and being severely chastised. Encouragement and good-humour are important in allowing a child to meet new experiences positively. If you encourage your child to expect the best from situations, their confidence will blossom.

One of the most common fears manifested by children at this stage is separation anxiety. Between one and two years of age, a toddler's most common response to being separated from his parent or regular carer is distress. It is only through the experience of the parent or carer returning that the child learns to handle separation. This fear of being left or separated is often combined with a suspicion of strangers. Both are entirely natural responses, and need to be handled with sensitivity. Often a child will simply grow out of this worry as he understands that the person he depends upon always returns, but in the meantime, it is important to explain to your toddler that you are leaving and will be coming back. To leave without saying goodbye can compound his anxiety, since it gives him no way of knowing when you might disappear. If he is being left at a nursery or daycare centre, it is reassuring for your departure to be the same each day. Children of this age are easily distracted and, providing they are being left in a suitable environment, they soon adapt to these experiences. I've always believed that a firm goodbye, a kiss and a hug, followed by a prompt departure is easiest for a child to deal with. He should not feel that he can delay your departure by becoming very upset. Toddlers are sensitive to parental anxiety, and it is important that on these occasions you do not demonstrate more than appropriate concern for their unhappiness, followed by a brief farewell.

Other common fears include the fear of water, often when the bath water is running away or the toilet flushing, and fear of the dark. Children of this age will sometimes become frightened of big bad animals, monsters and ghosts. These imaginary fears are very real when you are two and, again, need to be addressed sensitively. Recent research suggests that parents should not allow children under two to watch television. It is believed that toddlers who become used to the continual stimulation of television are unable to concentrate as effectively on real life, which is lived at a slower pace. Personally, I also believe that television can lead to fears in small children, due to the disturbing nature of some of even the most benign children's television. Addressing irrational fears in a pleasant way when your child is rested is a good way of dealing with their worries. Communicate with them, and help them to realise that there is nothing to be afraid of in a dark room or a cupboard. Also shield them from inappropriate influences such as television and computer games.

Some children develop a fear of certain people and places, such as policemen, doctors, hospitals and dentists. Role-playing can be an effective and fun way of helping them conquer these fears. Buy toys such as doctors and nurses kits, hairdressing kits, etc. to prepare your child for what happens when he has to visit the doctor or hairdresser. Read him books that involve happy stories of a child visiting the dentist or learning to swim. Familiarity is a great help for children of this age. If they have developed an idea of what to expect they are far more interested and less afraid of unusual experiences.

I try to encourage parents to be particularly careful to hide any adult phobia, since a fear of spiders or birds will be naturally copied by a small child. Perhaps the most exciting aspect of toddlerhood is your child's ability to assess, develop and respond to new situations. You will be his guide, and in every situation, from domestic to social, he will be evaluating and emulating the response of those around him.

Teaching toddlers about time

It is very difficult for children under three to grasp the concept of time. In order to help your child work towards an understanding of when certain things will be happening it is a good idea to introduce a picture calendar. This would be something very simple showing the days of the week split into morning and afternoon. You can then fill in the boxes with little pictures detailing what you and your child will be doing over the course of that week.

If you draw pictures of the things that you know your child likes most, this will encourage him to be more interested. It doesn't matter about the quality of the drawing; children of this age are rarely very critical.

Pre-school education

Between the ages of two and three, whether or not your child is already taking part in some form of childcare, you may find yourself considering pre-school education. This is usually available for all children from the age of two-and-a-half. Once your child reaches three years of age all approved pre-school education is state funded for a certain number of hours a week.

When deciding on pre-school education for your toddler it is worth spending time checking out and visiting several nurseries or playgroups to ensure that the one you choose is structured to meet your child's needs. Discuss in detail the school's discipline policy and whether they have regular parents' evenings or newsletters. It is also important to ensure that your child is ready emotionally, mentally and physically to attend nursery school. In my experience, a child who is used to being left with someone other than his parents for short periods will adapt to nursery much better than a child who has been cared for exclusively by his parents. I would suggest that several months before your child is about to start nursery you get him used to being left for short spells with either another family member or a good friend. Gradually increase the time he spends with them until he is happy to be separated from you for a period of three to four hours.

I have also observed that children who have been over-protected by parents have more difficulty adapting to the structure and rules within a nursery school environment. If your child is constantly looking for reassurance or refuses to co-operate with simple requests, it would be advisable to concentrate more on building up his self-esteem and confidence, as well as establishing very firm rules and limits so he understands obedience. Starting nursery or playgroup is a big step for a toddler, so the more you can do in the weeks prior to his first day, the easier he will find it to adapt.

The following suggestions will help make your child's start at nursery a happy time:

- Children of three years of age still have no concept of time, so avoid talking about nursery too far in advance. When the time to start gets closer it is worthwhile investing in some of the many available storybooks, that describe what happens when a child starts nursery.

- Arranging regular play dates with one or two other children who will be or are already attending the same nursery school can make things easier for your child. If you do not already know any parents in the area, ask the nursery school teacher if she can put you in touch with other parents who will be sending their child next term.

- Taking a child to nursery for the first time can be very emotional for some parents. Try not to let your child sense your anxiety when it comes to leaving him. The first few partings can often be made easier if you arrange with another mother to drop your children off together. Some nurseries encourage parents to stay with the children for a short period during the first week. This works for some children and not for others, and is worth discussing in advance with your nursery school teacher.

- Children who start off by attending nursery only one or two mornings a week and gradually build up the number of days are less likely to experience nursery fatigue. A child who has cut his afternoon nap and begins to display signs of becoming very overtired by the evening may need to have a short nap introduced again on the days he attends nursery.

- A child who has learned practical skills such as dressing, undressing and self-feeding and is completely potty trained will have a greater sense of independence and more confidence, making it easier to adapt to nursery, than a toddler who still relies on his mother to help him with these things.

- The first term at nursery can be both physically and mentally exhausting for a child. To ensure that your child does not suffer from nursery fatigue or become overtired at bedtime try to ensure that you start his bedtime routine a little earlier. A child between two and three years who is still having a nap in the afternoon would need to be in bed by 7.30pm. But a child who has dropped his nap altogether may need to be in bed by 7pm if he is to avoid becoming overtired. Remember that overtiredness is the main cause of bedtime battles and middle of the night wakings.

- Make sure that you spend a short time on your child's return from nursery discussing what has happened during the morning and which activities he has enjoyed most. Express how proud you are of his efforts to try new activities. If you notice that there are certain activities that he doesn't seem to enjoy, it is advisable to discuss with his teacher what you can do at home to make these activities more pleasurable.

Fear of separation from his mother can still be very strong for a child during the third year. Following the above guidelines and making sure that your child is emotionally, mentally and physically prepared for playgroup or nursery will prevent this becoming a problem.

Behaviour

The Word 'obedience', like 'discipline', will for many parents conjure up images of harshness and severity. During the second year allowances are made for the toddler because he has no real concept of right or wrong. However, as the toddler enters his third year nearly all parents expect some degree of obedience, and for many parents getting their toddler to do what he is told can become a real problem. Simple and reasonable requests such as 'clear your toys away', 'let's go upstairs for your bath', or 'take off your clothes' are all met with total resistance, and a battle of wills between parent and toddler usually ends up with him in tears, accused of being naughty and disobedient.

Jane Nelson says, 'A misbehaving child is a discouraged child, and we are more effective in redirecting the misbehaviour to positive behaviour when we remember the hidden message behind the behaviour. The misbehaving child is letting us know he does not think he has belonging and significance, and has mistaken beliefs about how to find belonging and significance.' She suggests that the best way to help a misbehaving child is through encouragement. When discouragement is removed, the motivation for misbehaviour will be gone. She quotes Rudolph Dreikurs, who helped develop Adlerian psychology: 'Children are good perceivers, but poor interpreters.' Nelson explains this further by saying that a child's behaviour will be based on what he believes to be true rather than on what is true.

I believe that much of the so-called disobedience and bad behaviour of young children is caused by parents sending out confusing signals. The following are my suggestions for improving your child's behaviour:

- Dreikurs said that 'Children need encouragement, just as plants need water. They cannot survive without it.' He believed that encouragement is one of the most important skills a parent can learn in helping their children. Try always to accentuate the positive and eliminate the negative by praising your child's strengths rather than commenting on his weaknesses. Expressing how pleased you are when he behaves well and reminding him of past times when he behaved well will do more to encourage good behaviour than reminding him of the times when he misbehaved.

- Grandparents who indulge children with presents and special treats are one thing, but on matters such as behaviour and manners they should follow your rules, otherwise it will only lead to your child becoming confused and to conflict within the family. A happy, relaxed family environment with a clear set of rules is more likely to result in a confident, well-behaved child than an environment that is filled with tension and conflict.

- Keeping to a fixed bedtime and routine will help to avoid a lack of cooperation. It is often inconsistency regarding rules and limits that confuses a child of less than three years and results in bad behaviour. I would advise sticking to set meal-times and avoiding later bedtimes. For example, changing mealtimes and allowing later bedtimes to fit in with visitors or because Daddy is at home is bound to confuse a child of under three years.

- Make sure that the rules and limits you are setting are appro-priate for your child's age and avoid having too many of them. Concentrate on obtaining your child's cooperation on important matters such as getting ready for bed, getting dressed, holding your hand in the street, etc. Avoid rules that involve your child sitting quietly for lengthy periods; for example, it is unfair to expect a child of less than three years of age to sit quietly through lengthy adult lunches. Likewise, a child of this age can be encouraged to help tidy his toys and clothes away, but he is too young to be expected always to take the initiative to do so himself.

- Children learn very quickly and if they are able to get away with bad behaviour in public they will use this to their advantage. If your child misbehaves in a shop or restaurant or at a friend's house, no matter how embarrassed you feel, it is better to deal with disobedience in public the same way you would at home.

- Make sure your child has heard and understands your request properly. All too often parents shout across the room to small children that lunch or tea will be ready in five minutes, and get cross when the child, who is engrossed in playing a certain game, refuses to come when called at the forewarned time. It is better to interrupt his play for a few minutes and get down to his level so he can see the expression on your face and hear clearly what you are saying. Ask him to repeat back to you what it is you expect him to do in five minutes. Sometimes setting a kitchen timer to buzz in five minutes helps act as a reminder. The use of a star chart can also be a very effective way of encouraging cooperation and good behaviour.

- A child of over two years old who is constantly in the buggy or car and not getting enough exercise and fresh air is more likely to be boisterous and noisy and get up to mischief around the home. All children benefit greatly from the opportunity to run around in the fresh air every day.

During the second year much of the toddler's so-called dis-obedient behaviour can be put down to frustration and lack of understanding between right and wrong; therefore punishment is not an issue. However, during the third year the child is beginning to have a greater understanding of what is expected of him and the difference between acceptable and unacceptable behaviour.

A parent who gets the balance right between building self-esteem, encouraging independence and teaching their child obedience should rarely have to resort to punishing their child. However, rare as these times are, it is important for parents to have discussed and mutually agreed in advance how bad beha-viour should be dealt with.

Q Our 22-month-old son is the only grandchild on both sides and adored by both sets of grandparents. The problem is that he is becoming increasingly more demanding and prone to having huge temper tantrums unless he gets what he wants immediately.

Both my husband and I have strict views about not over-indulging him with too many sweets and too much TV, but when either set of grandparents is around they think that it is acceptable to give in and allow him to have or do what he wants. They say that his ever-increasing bad behaviour is normal and all children go through this stage and that we are being mean by not allowing him to have sweets or watch TV every time he demands them. I now dread them coming to visit as they always come laden with several bags of sweets and new videos or toys, and by the time they leave he is so hyped up with eating junk food and being over-stimulated that it is a nightmare getting him to bed.

A Children are very discerning when it comes to knowing who is prepared to give in to them. There is nothing more frustrating for a parent than witnessing their structured approach to parenting being undermined by indulgent grandparents. When confronted with this dilemma I encourage the parents to talk to the grandparents. Choose a time when the child is in bed or otherwise occupied and when you are all relaxed. Make sure that your partner and the grandfather are there, so that it is not left for you to discuss it with your mother-in-law, since such discussion is then more likely to be viewed as criticism. Begin the discussion with a positive approach, commending the grandparents on their readiness to help with the grandchildren or their generosity. Then explain that you both feel that it would be really helpful if they cooperated with your wish for your child not to eat sweets. Explain that your concerns come from recent knowledge regarding the importance of avoiding too much sugar – one in five children under five have a rotten tooth or teeth. Describe how you feel that it adversely affects your child, stopping him eating a nutritious meal, and contributes to bad behaviour due to the effects of additives. It always helps to explain that you would like them to feel able to indulge their grandchild; however, this could take the form of extra bedtime stories or special play time rather than sweets. Most grandparents will understand if this is put to them in the right way. Explain that you feel your child has come to expect presents from his grandparents and that this is a shame since you would much prefer him to be excited at seeing them rather than at what they bring for him. Even if the grandparents are mildly offended, they will accept that this is the way you would like to bring up your child, and in time they too will see the benefits of a child who knows that whining and bad behaviour are not rewarded.

Punishment

All parents at some stage have to decide on appropriate punishments for the times when their child has been deliberately disobedient. Parents who are in disagreement over standards of behaviour and forms of punishment send conflicting signals to their child as to what is acceptable and what isn't. In my experience, these parents usually end up with a very manipulative and spoilt child.

During the third year, the first step a child will take towards becoming more independent of his parents is to attend nursery school. A child who has not learnt to cooperate with his parents at home will have a much more difficult time adapting to nursery school and taking instructions from other adults. All children will, from time to time, test their parents by being deliberately naughty, and some form of punishment may be needed.

Smacking

Twenty years ago a quick sharp smack was considered a fairly normal way of dealing with a disobedient child. Nowadays, childcare experts and parents are divided on whether smacking is an effective way of dealing with bad behaviour. Many child psychologists believe that smacking a child leads him to believe that violence is the way to deal with situations he can't control.

Smacking is already illegal in Austria, Finland, Denmark, Germany, Norway and Sweden, which might lead parents to consider seriously whether they should even consider it as a form of punishment. The UK government has so far resisted pressure to impose a ban on parents smacking their children, as they don't want to interfere 'in the normal course of family life'.

In my experience, the majority of parents who re.
smacking their child do so when they feel they are losing contr.
of a situation and their temper snaps. One of my clients who is
totally opposed to smacking walloped her four-year-old when he
deliberately pushed his 18-month-old sister into the duck pond in
Battersea Park, and another did the same when her three-year-old
daughter ran into the middle of a busy London street, bringing all
the traffic to a screeching halt.

In both of these instances I can understand why the mother
resorted to smacking and agree with Christopher Green's belief
that the minor emotional trauma caused by the smack is a small
price to pay if it prevents the major pain of injury and keeps
children alive and healthy. As he says, a smack might do more to
engrave the message on a toddler's mind that climbing onto the
edge of a high balcony is not allowed, than trying to debate
democratically with him that it is rather dangerous as it is 50
metres [160 feet] onto the road below and he might sustain a
nasty injury.

Only a very few of my clients have ever resorted to smacking
as a regular form of punishment for their children, and it is my
belief that as a punishment it rarely worked and only caused the
children to behave more aggressively. I believe that there are
other methods of punishment that are far more effective than
smacking. When deciding on a suitable form of punishment it is
essential that the one you choose is appropriate. For example,
with a child who throws his food on the floor or scribbles on the
wall it would be better to make him clean the mess up than to
make him take time out. Likewise, the child who loses his temper
and throws his toys around should have the toys in question
taken away for a short period. It is also important that the child
is given a warning of how he will be punished should he continue
to misbehave. A firm verbal warning given properly and in the
right manner can often eliminate the need for any further
punishment.

Verbal warning
When giving your child a verbal warning, it is essential that you
have his undivided attention. If he tries to run away from you it
is important that you restrain him by sitting him down in a chair
and holding his hands while you explain why you are unhappy

...dren under 36 months it is important to keep ...ple. All too often I hear parents getting more ...ght as they get trapped into lengthy discussions ...ing children of why something isn't acceptable. If ...anger element attached to the misbehaviour then it cei... should be explained to the child why they mustn't do a certain thing. But for misdemeanours such as jumping on the furniture, throwing his books or clothes on the floor etc., it is sometimes easier to say something like 'Mummy doesn't do that, Daddy doesn't do that and Tommy mustn't do that.' Try to avoid statements like 'Tommy is naughty and he mustn't do that.'

The tone of your voice and the look on your face will play a huge part in whether the warning is effective. All too often I hear reprimands sounding more like requests, which have little or no effect on the misbehaving child. I believe that without resorting to shouting you do need to raise your voice slightly, using the tone, along with the look in your eyes, to reflect how unhappy you are with your child's behaviour. A child must learn the consequence of his bad behaviour and it is important that you do not allow a verbal warning to turn into an empty threat. A child who is constantly threatened soon learns that his parents have no intention of punishing him and will become even more disobedient. If, despite giving your child a very firm warning, he continues to misbehave, the appropriate punishment should be administered immediately. Delaying the punishment for something he did several hours previously will only confuse him, as children under three years of age have not yet grasped the concept of time (please see page 39 for further information on teaching toddlers about time). Once he has been punished, the bad behaviour and punishment should not be mentioned again. Constantly reminding a child of his bad behaviour and using words such as 'naughty', 'nasty', 'clumsy', 'stupid' or 'silly' will not improve his behaviour and often leads to negative feelings about himself, causing him to be even more rebellious.

When a verbal reprimand does not have the desired effect, the two most effective punishments to choose from are either time out or withdrawal of a privilege. Which approach you take will depend very much on the age of your child and the reason for the bad behaviour.

Time out

In my experience a short spell of time out is the most effective way of dealing with misbehaviour. Children under three love to be on the move the whole time and in the company of others, which is why a short spell of solitude is the quickest way to calm down a child whose behaviour is getting out of control. It also teaches a child the consequences of breaking the rules and that he must take responsibility for his own actions.

Childcare experts are in disagreement as to where time out should take place. Many advise against using the bedroom in case the child comes to associate this room with punishment and fear, which could consequently cause sleep problems. It is often suggested that instead of the child's bedroom it is better to sit the child on the 'naughty' step or put them in the 'naughty' corner. In my experience this rarely works, and I agree with Richard Ferber that the bedroom is the best place. As he points out in his book *Solve Your Child's Sleep Problems*, 'If putting a toddler in his bedroom will put him off sleeping, then presumably putting him in the bathroom will put him off washing, the dining room off eating, the lounge off sitting, the kitchen off dishwashing and so on. I choose the bedroom because it is sufficiently soundproof and far enough away from the rest of the house to give both parties the space they need to calm down.'

A disobedient child who ignores a verbal warning should be taken to his bedroom immediately before things get totally out of control. Having decided on this course of action it is essential that you carry it out quickly and calmly. The child who protests and screams should, if necessary, be picked up and carried there. The sooner you get your child to his room and leave him there the quicker he will calm down and the less likely you will be to lose control yourself and resort to shouting, arguing or nagging, which is what usually happens when parents keep trying to reason with a distraught and disobedient child.

The purpose of time out is to give your child the opportunity to calm down and realise how much more pleasurable life is when spent in the company of others and that bad behaviour in the company of others is not tolerated. Leaving him alone and reminding him that you will return the minute he has calmed down is the quickest way to achieve this. However, I do not think there is any great benefit in leaving a small child upset and alone for lengthy periods, as it usually results in the child becoming hysterical and trashing the room. I would allow a period of between three and five minutes and if he hadn't calmed down I would return to the room and remind him that he would be allowed out if he was ready to behave. The answer is nearly always 'yes'. Therefore I would bring him out, but should he start misbehaving again I would repeat the whole procedure. With some children the procedure has to be repeated many, many times, but eventually they learn that an ignored warning of bad behaviour will always result in them being taken to their room.

Withdrawal of privileges

A simplified version of withdrawal of privileges can be used as the child approaches his third birthday. Because a child of this age still does not have much awareness of time, the withdrawal of the privilege must happen immediately. Restricting a video in the evening or cancelling a trip to the playground in the afternoon because he misbehaved in the morning will not be effective. However, there are certain occasions when a child is misbehaving that an immediate withdrawal of a privilege can work. For example, a child who is deliberately being destructive with a toy or book, or who scribbles all over the kitchen table should have the item in question removed for the remainder of the day. Likewise, the child who insists on running around while eating a biscuit should have the biscuit taken away, and the child who misbehaves at a play date can be taken home.

As with time out, the child should always be given a verbal warning of what will happen if he continues to misbehave. If you find you constantly have to reprimand or punish your child for deliberate misbehaviour, it is essential that you look closely at both the reasons for the misbehaviour and at the form of punishments you are using. It is also worthwhile discussing any worries you may have about your child's behaviour with your health visitor, who will be able to reassure you as to whether or not your concerns have any foundation.

Gemma, aged 27 months

Lucinda, mother of Gemma, aged 27 months, and George, aged three months, was at breaking point when she contacted me for help. She was finding it very difficult coping with both children on her own (her husband left very early in the morning and often had to work late in the evening) and had become so depressed about the whole situation that her doctor had prescribed anti-depressants. I agreed to spend a week with the family to help get George into a routine.

On the evening of my arrival Lucinda explained her dilemma to me more fully. George was waking and feeding three or four times a night and fretful most of the day. While Gemma didn't wake in the middle of the night, she was difficult to settle at bedtime, often not falling asleep until 10 or 11pm. Since the arrival of her brother, Gemma had refused to take her midday nap and was prone to several temper tantrums a day.

Although my role as a maternity nurse was to establish a feeding and sleeping routine for George, I felt so sorry for Lucinda that I suggested she have a complete break from both children, and take the whole of the following day off. I know that depression can make a problem appear much worse than it really is, and I confidently assured Lucinda that I could easily cope with both children for the day.

The following morning after Gemma, George and I had waved goodbye to a very anxious Lucinda, I sat down and explained to my two angelic-looking charges what an exciting day we were all going to have. Finger painting, colouring, cookie making and a picnic in the park were just a few of the activities I had planned.

By 5pm that evening I fully understood why Lucinda had looked so anxious on her departure that morning. Within a few hours I had gone from being a calm, confident expert on childcare to a gibbering wreck. My plan for a day packed with enjoyable activities had ended up with the cream-coloured damask-covered sofa covered in bright red paint. The colouring session finished with Gemma trying to shove a jumbo green crayon into George's mouth, and during the picnic in the park Gemma somehow managed to get the lid off her any-way-up cup and drown George in apple juice. To protect George from Gemma's frequent attacks, *he was constantly carried and held, instead of kicking under the play-gym as I usually recommend. Neither child slept a wink during the day, and by bath time both were screaming hysterically. Trying to get them both upstairs that evening was a bit like trying to scale Mount Everest with two screeching baby chimpanzees attached to my back. My plans for structuring George's feeds had also gone out of the window – later that evening I counted no less than eight bottles of half-finished milk.*

That night I made a silent vow that no matter how desperate or depressed a mother was, I would never again offer to help out with the elder siblings of my babies. For the remainder of the week I concentrated on structuring George's feeding and sleeping problems, and by the end of the week he was in a good routine, happy and content during the day, settling well at 7pm, feeding at 11pm and sleeping through until 6.45am. However, from my observations of the struggle Lucinda was having trying to cope with Gemma's tantrums, the food fights at mealtimes and battles at bedtimes, I doubted that Lucinda would have the time and the energy needed to keep George in the routine.

This proved to be true, as only days after my departure I received a hysterical telephone call from Lucinda, begging me to come back for a further week, as George had started to wake up in the night again. Trying to be tactful, I explained to Lucinda that it really would be pointless because it wasn't George who had the problem. He was one of the least demanding babies I had cared for, but even very easy babies require time and attention if any sort of routine is to be maintained. This was impossible in Lucinda's case because coping with Gemma's demanding and difficult behaviour left her very little time for George.

The sobbing Lucinda became so upset that I agreed to go back for a further week, on the condition that we sorted out Gemma's behaviour.

That evening I sat down with both parents to discuss how we could best improve Gemma's behaviour. From the observations that I had made of Gemma the previous week it was my belief that one of the main causes was their inconsistent approach to dealing with her disobedience, particularly at mealtimes and bedtimes. The following list pinpoints the main causes of Gemma's extreme disobedience, and shows the suggestions I made for her parents to improve the situation.

Bedtimes

- *I believed that a major cause of Gemma's bad behaviour during the day was her very late bedtime. Recent research shows that children of Gemma's age who are getting less than 10 hours sleep at night are more prone to aggressive or bad behaviour. I advised that Gemma's bedtime should be brought forward using the late bedtime plan on page 33. Over a two-week period her parents managed gradually to bring her bedtime forward until eventually she was happily settling at 7.30pm.*

- *Gemma's inconsistent bedtime routine was the main reason she ended up fighting sleep and going to bed late. The inconsistency stemmed from the fact that her parents each followed a different approach to putting her to bed. Two or three evenings a week Gemma's father managed to get home early to put her to bed and, despite pleas from Lucinda, he would immediately get involved with some boisterous activity or game with Gemma. When the time came for her bath Gemma would be so hyped up that her father had to invent another game to get her upstairs. He would pretend to be an aeroplane and with Gemma perched on his shoulders would run around the house before eventually running up the stairs to the bathroom. The fun and games would continue right through the bath and while Gemma was getting dressed. Although she was perfectly capable of getting herself dressed and undressed, Gemma would be so overexcited that her father would end up doing it for her. All of this would take so long that it meant that Gemma was rarely in bed before 8.30pm. She would be so excited that she was unable to settle, demanding more and more stories, another drink of milk or one last cuddle from Daddy. It could often take a further two hours before she would go to sleep. On the evenings that Lucinda was by herself, running around after tea and flying Gemma upstairs on her shoulders was impossible as she also had the baby to deal with. Gemma, expecting but not getting the same fun and games she had on the nights Daddy put her to bed, would soon resort to tears and tantrums to get her way. Bath time and bedtime usually ended up with Gemma crying and refusing to settle. Lucinda would become so stressed trying to cope with both children that she would soon also be in tears.*

I wrote down the following list of guidelines that had to be followed every night regardless of which parent was putting Gemma to bed:

- *There should be no boisterous games or activities after tea that would cause Gemma to become overexcited. The 15-minute time gap after tea and before the bath should be spent with either one or both parents encouraging and helping Gemma to get into the habit of tidying her toys away. A star chart was used as an incentive to get Gemma to do this.*

- *When it was time to go upstairs for the bath Gemma was to be given two choices. She could hold either one of her parents' hands and climb the stairs quickly and quietly, for which she would receive a further star, or she could be carried up without fun or fuss and put in the cot while her parents went back down to get the baby. It was important that on the night both parents put the children to bed together they still used the same approach. Gemma had to make an immediate decision, without coaxing or cajoling. On the nights she tried to provoke her father into playing on the stairs, she was to be picked up immediately and without comment taken upstairs and put in her cot until the baby was also brought up. While the bath was being run, Gemma was to be encouraged to undress herself and would receive a further star when she attempted to take off most of her clothes. If Gemma tidied her toys away, climbed the stairs quickly and attempted to undress, she would be allowed to put three stars on the chart that hung on her bedroom door. A total of three stars were rewarded with a treat: special bubbles in her bath.*

Mealtimes
- *Mealtimes were another major problem for Gemma's parents, but here they did both take the same approach. When Gemma played up and refused to eat, both parents would resort to spoon-feeding her, which usually ended up with Gemma in tears as they forced spoonfuls of food down her throat. From my observations of Gemma at mealtimes it was obvious that being allowed to drink an excessive amount of juice in between meals and while eating was a major cause of her lack of appetite. That combined with the unrealistic amount of*

food her parents expected her to eat resulted in constant battles at mealtimes. I advised her parents to restrict her juice intake to mealtimes only. The juice should then be very well diluted and not put on the table until she had eaten at least half of her food, and in between meals she should be given only water. I also suggested that they should put only the smallest amount of food on her plate, for example half a chopped-up fish finger, served with one tiny diced potato, one floret of cauliflower and one teaspoonful of peas. She was then to be left alone in peace to eat this, with no coaxing or cajoling. Once she finished this she was to be allowed a small drink of very well diluted juice before being offered another small selection of food. If she didn't eat well at one meal she was not to be allowed to fill up on snacks before the next one. While Gemma still continued to be faddy about certain foods, this approach led to a huge improvement in the total amount she would eat over several mealtimes. Seeing that Gemma could eat reasonable amounts at some mealtimes gave her parents the courage to leave her to decide on how much she should eat at individual meals.

Routine
- *Lucinda thought she had done all the right things to prepare Gemma for the arrival of her baby brother. Although she had anticipated some degree of jealousy after the birth, she was not prepared for Gemma's unpredictable behaviour. At times she could be very loving towards the baby, attempting to kiss and cuddle him, then suddenly, for no apparent reason, she would become very aggressive, trying to hit or scratch him. In my experience, this type of behaviour is more common when there is no set routine for a second baby. A baby who is fed on demand and carried from room to room in his Moses basket is bound to represent more of a threat to the elder child. Lucinda was constantly telling Gemma off for going too near the baby or for making too much noise when he was asleep. Once Lucinda began to stick rigidly to the routine I had set for George and put him to sleep at nap times in the nursery it made it easier for her to give Gemma individual attention on a regular basis. I also suggested that when Gemma went to touch the baby they encouraged her to tickle his feet, saying*

how much George liked the way she tickled his toes. This form of diverting Gemma's desire constantly to touch him was much better than reprimanding her for trying to touch his head.

Within days of her parents following my advice Gemma was like a different child, happy during the day and settling well at bedtime. Her eating improved dramatically and she was no longer aggressive towards George. I believe that many of the jealousy problems could have been avoided if both parents had encouraged Gemma to learn more skills before the arrival of her brother. This would have encouraged her to be more independent and not so reliant on her mother.

Lucinda had no close family at hand to help out with the children. I feel she would have found coping with two children easier if she had got Gemma used to attending a playgroup or nursery once or twice a week. I believe that most children of between two and three years of age benefit enormously from attending a nursery school or organised playgroup as it teaches them how to share and participate in group activities. I find that children who have learned these two important skills are also more confident and independent and less likely to resent the arrival of a new baby brother or sister.

Social skills

A lack of manners and not wanting to share are the two things that the majority of parents are concerned about during the third year. All parents want their child to be polite and show kindness and sensitivity towards other people, but because children under three years are still very self-centred they will need constant reminders while learning these social skills.

The more a child is taught to take responsibility for his own actions, and so to understand the consequences of unacceptable behaviour, the easier it will be for him to learn to be polite and respectful of others' feelings.

The following sections give advice on how to encourage your child to be well mannered and respectful.

Please and thank you

By the age of two years most children have a good comprehension of what is being said to them, even if their vocabulary is still fairly limited. It is important, therefore, that you always remember to use 'please' and 'thank you' yourself when talking to your child. During the first half of the third year your child will need constant reminders to say 'please' and 'thank you', but as he approaches his third birthday he should need reminding less often. If your child reaches three years of age and you are regularly having to say 'What's the magic word?' a different approach may be needed. Completely ignoring the request of a child who forgets to say 'please' will quickly teach him to remember to say it; likewise, not letting go of something your child has asked for until he has said 'thank you' will teach him the importance of these words. During the third year you should also encourage your child to draw pictures to send as thank you letters for gifts he has received from family and friends, or when he has attended birthday parties or other events.

Table manners

Because of the hectic lifestyle we all lead nowadays, eating as a family is often the exception rather than the rule, and the first impression children frequently have of social eating is watching their parents munching on a sandwich or ready-made meal while trying to do other tasks. If you are not already doing so, try to eat at least one meal a day with your toddler. This is the best way to encourage good table manners, as toddlers learn best by example. A child who observes the courtesy and appreciation of the sharing of a meal between his parents will be much more likely to learn good table manners at a young age. I have witnessed three-year-olds who would always say 'please' and 'thank you', and comment on how nice the food was, and I have also witnessed five-year-olds who still have to be reminded to say 'please' and 'thank you', and would have no qualms about turning their nose up and rudely announcing that the food was yuck. I never had to look very far to see how these children learned their table manners!

A child who eats well and enjoys mealtimes will learn good table manners much quicker than the child who eats poorly. Trying to instil too many rules at one time can cause further eating problems for a child who is already eating poorly. Try to make mealtimes as happy and relaxed as possible and avoid possible distractions such as having the television set on.

During the third year, eating becomes less messy and a child will have learnt that the throwing and spilling of food is unacceptable. While occasional mishaps should be overlooked, a child who deliberately spills or drops food should be reprimanded. However, reprimanding a child of this age for eating with his mouth open, not putting his cup down between sips or leaning his elbows on the table would be completely unreasonable.

While your child does need to learn the difference between good and bad table manners, it is unfair to expect him to be able to concentrate on learning all these skills at the same time, so work on one skill at a time. Once he begins to master a particular skill, such as putting his cup down between sips, eating with his mouth closed or not talking with his mouth full, give him lots of praise. Having at least some of the food served from a central plate is also a great way of encouraging good manners and teaching your toddler to share. The passing of food between you and your partner accompanied by 'please' and 'thank you' and verbal expression of how good it tastes will set an example of what is eventually expected of your toddler. Discussing the shape, size and colour of different foods will also help him to learn verbal skills. With older children this information can be expanded to how the different foods are grown and which country they come from. Discussion at mealtimes makes eating more interesting and enjoyable and is all part of your child learning the art of social eating, but it is important to remember not to ask your toddler questions while he is actually eating his food. Wait until he has finished a mouthful before engaging him in conversation. This will eventually teach him that talking with his mouth full is rude, provided of course that he doesn't observe you talking with your mouth full.

Q My two-and-a-half-year-old son who used to be very well behaved at mealtimes accidentally knocked his juice off the table while we were having tea with his grandparents. His grandmother is quite old-fashioned and strict and gave him a very stern look and told him he was naughty, which resulted in him bursting into tears. I felt that it was a genuine accident and that he should not have been reprimanded for it. He is a very sensitive little boy and I immediately went to comfort him as he was becoming increasingly distraught. A full-blown row evolved over the issue, and to make matters worse my husband agreed with his mother. She maintains that at his age he should have known to have been more careful.

Since then mealtimes have become a nightmare, particularly when my husband is present, as he constantly reminds our son to be careful when eating and drinking. My son is now constantly spilling his juice or knocking his food over, and my husband says that he is just being naughty and doing it to seek attention. I really am unsure whether this behaviour is because he is getting stressed at mealtimes or because he really is being naughty. How do I know what is causing this sudden change in behaviour?

A I certainly agree with you that your mother-in-law dealt with the accident in the wrong way. But your son is always going to meet people who have stricter rules about certain things and it is important that he learns how to deal with people who handle a situation differently from that of his parents. I think that you were right to comfort your son, but it would have been better in the long run to get him to apologise to Granny and say that he would try not to do it again than get into a row with your mother-in-law. Once you had left you could always have reassured your son a bit more while making light of the situation – 'Granny is a bit strict, isn't she? Mummy's granny used to be just the same when Mummy spilt her juice. We'll just have to be more careful the next time we go to Granny's.'

Unfortunately, so much emphasis has been placed on the incident that it is difficult to work out whether your son's behaviour at the table is now caused because by genuine stress about eating and drinking or whether it is actually to get attention. Possibly it is a bit of both, and my advice would be that when he does spill his drink or drop his food on the floor, both you and your husband remain very calm and say something like, 'Oh dear, that's a shame. You've spilt your juice. Mummy will get a cloth and we will clean it up together.' If he protests, be sympathetic about the accident but firm and insistent about him helping clean it up. If necessary, you could explain that Mummy's back is very sore today and she can't reach the floor, so he will have to do it by himself. If you persist, he will eventually understand that you and his father are not going to overreact to his behaviour with either excessive annoyance or excessive sympathy and that his actions do have consequences for which he has to take the responsibility. It would also be a good idea to implement a star chart so that he gets a star every time he manages to eat and drink at a meal without an accident. After he has several stars in a column he could be given a special dessert or ice cream as a reward. But do remember that rewards should only be given as a result of good behaviour and not offered before as a form of bribery.

Interrupting

Teaching a child under three years of age that it is bad manners to interrupt you while you are having a conversation with a friend or talking on the phone is virtually impossible. As already discussed, before the age of three years children do not fully understand the concept of time and therefore can't grasp what waiting a few minutes really means. The majority of parents that I know with children of this age openly admit to bribery when they need to make an urgent phone call or have an important conversation with someone. Allowing their child to watch a video or giving a drink or juice and a biscuit usually guarantees 10 minutes of uninterrupted conversation time.

Like the majority of social skills, this one is learnt best by example. Approaching your child politely when you require his attention will go a long way towards helping him learn not to interrupt rudely.

If your child is playing with a friend and you wish to talk to him, get his attention in the same respectful way you would another adult. Do not shout a command or question across the room; go to where he is playing or talking and stoop slightly to his level to make eye contact. Try to use the same simple gesture each time you want his attention. Once you have his full attention you can make your request.

Likewise, when he wants your attention, respond appropriately. By using the same signal when you want his attention and encouraging him to do the same when he wants yours you will soon teach him to wait a minute or two until you have finished talking.

Dressing

During the third year all children are capable of undressing and dressing themselves, apart from buttons and zips. Continuing to do these things for your child because it is quicker will do little to help his growing independence. Allow extra time at mealtimes and in the morning and evening so you have the patience to guide him and encourage him to do these things for himself.

Your toddler will be less likely to get frustrated or bored if you teach him to undress and dress in stages. Once he is capable of taking off his socks and trousers, move on to him taking off his socks, trousers and pants, etc. Use the same approach when teaching him how to dress himself. You can encourage his independence by allowing him to choose which clothes he wears, but do limit the choice so that you remain in control.

Q My two-and-a-half-year-old son refuses to get dressed himself and so I generally resort to doing it myself to save time. How should I get him to take more responsibility for himself?

A Children of this age tend to be more receptive to learning new skills during the day, so I would suggest that you begin by choosing a regular time once or twice a week when things aren't so pressurised. For instance, if your child still has a lunchtime nap, when he wakes up keep him from going downstairs until he has put on his trousers himself. As his skills increase, I would gradually build up to getting him to dress himself fully before he can carry on with the afternoon. Without the pressures of the school run or even just breakfast, both you and your child can tackle the task with calm and resolve. If you promise a trip the swings or a walk this can often add to the incentive.

If your child isn't sleeping during the day I would still use the time after lunch as 'quiet time' (see page 62). In this case I would persuade him that he can have a story read to him if he gets into bed in just his under things. Then if he doesn't need a sleep I would say something along the lines of, 'Big boys who don't need lunchtime sleeps can get dressed themselves.' Then I would persuade him to start with just one item of clothing and gradually over the weeks build up to a situation where he is getting fully dressed by himself.

Sleep

Although children between the ages of two and three tend to reduce the amount of time they spend sleeping, it is still very important to ensure that they are getting at least 10 or more hours sleep a night. Recent research shows that children who sleep for less than 10 hours a night are more prone to aggressive or bad behaviour. Often, just putting your child to bed half an hour earlier than normal can result in them sleeping an extra half an hour in the night.

Dropping the lunchtime sleep and introducing quiet time

If your child is between the ages of two and three and seems not to need a sleep in the afternoon, I would still recommend taking him up to his bedroom after lunch and trying to get him to read a book or play quietly with his toys. It is important for all the family that there is at least one time during the normal day when both you and your children can be quiet. Even if your child refuses to go to his room I would still insist that during this hour there is no running and shouting in the house. Obviously, if you have friends over or are out and about then this isn't practical, but during an ordinary day I generally find mothers welcome a little time out. Often I find that children who seem to have given up sleeping during the day will, if given the opportunity of quiet time, fall asleep at least once or twice a week. This extra hour can greatly improve the general behaviour of a child as it stops overtiredness setting in towards the end of the week.

Transferring your toddler to the big bed

I always recommend leaving your toddler in a cot until they are between two-and-a-half and three years of age. If you are expecting another child and need to be able to accommodate both children, I would encourage you to borrow a second cot from a friend. Advice these days is always to invest in a new mattress for a new baby, so ideally the toddler would keep his mattress in the borrowed cot. I do feel that the toddler has a great deal to adjust to with the arrival of a new baby, and this is not the best time to be embarking on the experience of a new bed too. If you have just had a baby, try to wait until the new baby is a few months old before moving him to a bed. However, I would advise that your toddler sleeps in a sleeping bag while still in his cot as this will ensure that the possibility of him trying to climb out never arises.

When the time does come to transfer your toddler to a big bed, if you have the space, begin by introducing the new bed into your toddler's room while he is still in his cot. This will enable the toddler to get used to climbing up on the bed for his bedtime story and a cuddle.

If you don't have the room and you need to swap the bed for the cot, it is a good idea to spend a week or two discussing it with your toddler and make it an exciting adventure. Now and again I have come across children who are really attached to their cot and find the loss of it threatening. If you think this might be the case with your child, it would be a good idea to spend more time preparing him for the change. Take him to help choose the bed linen.

When asked to recommend a particular style of bed, I tend to encourage mothers to invest in a proper adult-sized single bed, although it is sensible to get one that is low to the floor. Cots that convert into cot beds are popular. The disadvantage of these is that you tend to need the cot for the new baby, so the benefits and saving of having a cot that converts to a bed are lost unless you are intending to buy a second cot. It is also more difficult to get standard bed linen for cot beds. Investing in an adult single bed means that you don't have to buy another bed when your child is five. I wouldn't buy an expensive mattress initially. Most mattress suppliers offer an inexpensive single mattress and this can be upgraded once your child is beyond bed-wetting.

I advise using a detachable bed rail for the first few months in the new bed, as this will prevent toddlers from rolling out of bed. The best of these will be made of cotton mesh on a soft-padded frame. I am not a fan of bunk beds since I know of too many incidents of children falling from them, and also I don't think they are very conducive to reading bedtime stories and having goodnight cuddles.

Another method of introducing your child to sleeping in a big bed is to organise a trip away where there will be no cot available. This way you can let your toddler sleep in a big bed away from home and then when you get back show him his new bed in his bedroom.

If you have a toddler whose excitement at sleeping in a new bed disrupts bedtime, I would suggest using a stair gate on the bedroom door. I would fix this a few inches above the floor so that your toddler cannot climb over it. One of the most common reasons for a child waking in the night in his new bed is because he is cold. I would recommend clasps that secure the bed linen to the bed and prevent the sheets falling off.

Bedtime battles

The toddler who refuses to go to bed is a very common problem. What used to be a calm and happy event can very quickly resemble a battleground, with all parties feeling tired and exhausted. The question and answer below gives a clear picture of how I would approach this situation.

Q We transferred our three-year-old daughter from her cot to a bed over six months ago, four months before her baby sister was born. She adapted happily to her bed and we did not experience any of the problems of getting out of bed that many parents describe.

   However, since the birth of her sister two months ago, she has started to resist bedtime more and more. She used to settle in her bed easily by 7.30pm every night and was usually asleep within 10 minutes. Now she keeps getting out of bed and running around upstairs, shouting for another drink or a story, or saying that she is frightened of the monsters. It can take up to two hours to get her to calm down and go off to sleep, during which time the noise she makes usually ends up waking the baby, which is throwing her routine out as well.

A This is a very common problem that I had to deal with a lot when I worked as a maternity nurse. If you are very patient and consistent it is possible to resolve it without lots of fuss or crying. The first thing to aim for is to get your toddler to stay happily in her bed in the evening. Once you have achieved this you will find that she will gradually return to getting herself off to sleep around 7.30pm. The important thing is not to keep telling her that she must go to sleep, as this is the surest way of encouraging her to play up and want your attention. Instead, when you finish reading her final bedtime story, tell her that you are just popping to get something from your bedroom. If she stays in her bed and quietly reads her book or listens to her music tape, you will leave her bedside light on and the door open. However, if she jumps out of bed and makes a noise, the door will be closed and the light turned off. You then leave the room for no more than 30 seconds, stand just outside her door and remind her that you will be back in a minute if she stays in bed, but if she gets out of bed you will not come back into the room, and the door will be shut and the light turned off. It is important to return to the room within half a minute so that she does not have time to get out of the bed. When you return tell her how clever she has been staying in her bed and ask her what the story is about, but under no circumstances go back to sitting by the bed or reading a further story. Instead, pretend to tidy a cupboard or drawer, then after a couple of minutes make a further excuse to leave the room. Repeating the same warning as before, again stand outside the door and reassure her that you will be back if she stays quietly in her bed. Extend the time to one minute before returning and repeating the same procedure as before. Keep repeating the same procedure of entering and leaving the room, gradually extending the time that you are out of the room. It can take several nights to build up the time that you are out of the room, but if you are patient you will reach a stage where you are out of the room for 15–20 minutes at a time.

Once this stage has been reached I used to find that I would often go back in and the toddler would have fallen asleep while reading their book. I would always praise them in the morning and put a sticker on their chart if they had stayed in bed. I would also always remind them that when I turned off or dimmed the light I gave them a very big kiss goodnight.

The key to this working is not to extend the time that you are outside the door too quickly, as this will give your daughter the opportunity to get out of the bed, which is what you are aiming to avoid. Obviously, if she gets out of the bed you must immediately put her back into bed, switch the light off and close the door. She will get upset and may try to open the door, so you will have to hold the handle so she can't get out.

Do not get into conversations other than to remind her that once she gets back into bed and promises to stay there, you will then turn the light on and she can go back to reading her book or listening to her music tape.

This method never failed when I had to use it, and rarely did I have any screaming or crying while doing it, but be prepared for it to take up to a couple of weeks to work.

Early morning waking

Whether a child will be an early morning waker is very much dictated by what happens during the first year. I have found that children who as babies were put to bed late and did not have proper established naps during the day are much more likely to become early morning wakers, expecting to start the day often as early as 5am.

Sometimes, however, early morning walking can also become a problem when a child who has always slept well is transferred from his cot to a bed, usually some time during the third year. With a child who has always slept well the problem is much easier to solve than with a child who, over a long period of time, has got into the habit of waking. There are also some children who do need less sleep, and it is unrealistic to expect them to sleep longer or to get angry with them. They can learn, however, that when they wake up they must wait quietly until you go and get them up. By being firm and consistent and never getting into a conversation with a child who wakes early you can teach them not to shout or fuss when they wake up. Remember, the aim is to get your child either to lie quietly in bed listening to a tape or to play quietly with his toys, not necessarily to go back to sleep. Whichever one he chooses to do, it should be done in a dimly lit room; on no account should a big light be put on or the curtains opened. These two things should only be done when you go to get him up, as he will eventually learn that these two cues signal the start of the day.

The following are guidelines on how to deal with a child who is waking early:

- If your child is able to open his bedroom door, it is worthwhile considering putting up a stair gate on the door. Once children learn that they are unable to get out of the room they are much more inclined to climb back into bed, especially if the room is very dark. Parents should remember that there is also a safety issue to consider when a young child is able to get out of his room and wander around the house. Many years ago, I came face-to-face one morning with a three-year-old at the top of the stairs holding his three-week-old sister in his arms. I had gone downstairs to get the formula and in the meantime the baby had woken up. Because the toddler was able to open all the doors, he had decided to go and give the baby a cuddle. I shudder to think what would have happened if he had attempted to go down the stairs while carrying the baby. From that day on I took bookings only where the families had stair gates on both the baby's and the toddler's room doors.
- I believe that a very dark room is just as important for a toddler and young child as it is for a baby. To my knowledge not one of the 300 babies I have helped care for has ever got up before 7am. As they get older, some may wake at 6–6.30am, but the parents tell me that after a short spell of singing or chattering to themselves they usually go back to sleep until 7.30am. I am convinced that the reason for this is that they are all used to sleeping in very dark rooms, with the door shut.
- If a child develops a fear of the dark, he should not be forced to sleep in pitch darkness. It is much better to use a plug-in low voltage night-light than to leave the door open, as the latter encourages the child to get up, expecting to start the day.
- A child who wakes up before 6am and gets out of bed expecting to start the day should be put straight back to bed and told simply and firmly, 'It's not time to get up yet.' It is important not to get into discussions of any sort. If you are consistent enough and follow it through no matter how often he gets out of bed, this method will eventually work. If he is in

the habit of getting up and asking for a drink, make sure that a small beaker of water is always left by his bedside.

- Many parents claim that using a bunny alarm clock helps to prevent their child from expecting to start the day too early. The clock is designed to look like a bunny's face and has eyes that open and shut, which are operated by an alarm mechanism. At night the parents set the alarm for the time their child is allowed out of his room in the morning. The eyes of the bunny then shut and only open up again at the time for which they have set the alarm. I find that giving the child a star on his chart for the mornings he waited until the bunny's eyes opened before calling out can sometimes be a big incentive. However, I feel I should mention that some very determined children quickly learn how to operate the clock and manage to get the eyes open long before the time for which it was set!

- A child who is waking nearer to 6.30am and getting out of bed should not be forced to go back to bed, but he can learn to play quietly in his room with his toys until the bunny's eyes open. Sometimes pre-setting a cassette recorder to play a nursery rhyme tape around the time the child usually wakes can encourage him to stay in his bed. Again, he can be rewarded with a star on his chart on the days he does remain quiet.

Fear of the dark

During the third year even the most happy and confident child can develop a fear of the dark. A child who suddenly starts becoming fretful and frightened at bedtime and talking of monsters being in the room should be taken seriously. At this age he is still unable to comprehend the difference between what is real and what isn't, so telling him not to be silly and that monsters do not exist will be of no help. Dr Miriam Stoppard says, 'If your child is afraid of monsters or ghosts say that you are a parent who can do magical things to them. Say that you are able to blow them away and give a big blow.' I have found this sort of approach far more effective than trying to convince the child the monster doesn't exist. Giving your child a special magic toy that sits near the door to keep the monsters out can also be a successful way of eliminating a child's fears.

Some parents tell me that leaving a small plug-in light on until the child goes to sleep can also be reassuring. If a child starts to wake up frightened in the night or have nightmares it would be advisable to leave it on all night. This in my mind is better than leaving the door open. Problems can often arise when a second baby comes along if the elder child is used to having the door open, as they are more inclined to get up in the night if they hear their mother attending to the baby.

Q Our four-year-old son, who has always slept in the dark with the room door shut, is now demanding to have the door open and the light on, saying that he is frightened of the monsters. My husband insists that he is being silly, that monsters only exist in storybooks and that big boys don't need to sleep with the light on. It is becoming a real issue and he is taking longer and longer to settle at bedtime. We end up having to go back in to him several times during the evening, and he is often not falling asleep until nearly 9pm. This is resulting in him getting very tired during the day, and his nursery school has commented that he is not the happy little relaxed boy he used to be. With a new baby on the way I am desperate to try and resolve this problem before the baby arrives.

A It is very common for toddlers and young children to develop a fear of the dark, and I think it can be very damaging to force a child of this age to try to face up to his fears and force him to go to sleep in the dark. I think that many children of this age do develop certain fears and often are not really aware of what they are frightened of, using monsters as a reason for not wanting to be alone.

The ongoing battle to get your son to go to sleep in the dark is creating a bedtime sleeping problem which, if allowed to continue, will in the long term be much harder to resolve than his fear of the dark.

Instead of dismissing your little boy's fears as silly, I would suggest that you give him lots of reassurance that Mummy and Daddy are just next door. You can either leave a small night-light on in his room, with the door closed, or you can leave his room door slightly open with a dim light from the hall to reassure him. Obviously, it would be better if he could be persuaded to settle for a night-light in his room, so that his

ɔor could be closed, rather than leaving the door open with
a hall light on, which could lead to the problem of him being
woken in the night when the baby wakes.

Using a star chart to reward him when he settles quickly
and easily in the evening will also help.

Nightmares

The majority of childcare experts claim that nightmares before
the age of three years are very rare. Dr Richard Ferber appears to
disagree with these claims. He says that 'dreams, and even
nightmares, unquestionably do occur during the second year of
life'. Ferber believes that nightmares are mainly a symptom of
daytime emotional struggles. He says that 'although most
nightmares do reflect emotional conflicts, in most cases neither
the nightmares nor the conflicts are "abnormal". Rather, the
normal emotional struggles associated with growing up are at
times significant enough to lead to occasional nightmares.'

Having been woken in the middle of the night many times
over the years by the screams of the elder siblings of my babies,
I would have to agree with Ferber's view. Nearly all of these
children were between 18 months and three years, and those
able to talk would, once calmed down, be able to describe the
nightmare.

Although all the experts are in agreement that a child who has
had a nightmare should immediately be comforted and reassured,
opinion is divided on whether nightmares can be controlled or
not. Dr John Pearce, author of *The New Baby and Toddler Sleep
Programme*, believes that because nightmares occur in the
lightest stages of sleep, they can often be controlled. He explains
that because a child's imagination is more adaptable than an
adult's, it is more open to suggestion. He advises that parents
work out a plan for how to deal with the monster, for example
making the monster fall into a hole, drown or get trapped in a
cage.

I personally find that this approach works much better than
trying to convince the child there isn't a monster. Often I have
heard a young child getting more and more upset as their parents
insist on trying to convince them that the monster isn't real. This
happens because a child under three years of age who wakes up

frightened by a nightmare is not yet able to grasp the difference between dreaming and reality.

I have also observed that those elder siblings of my babies who have suffered from nightmares nearly all had inconsistent bedtime routines or had previously experienced sleeping problems. It is interesting that very few of the babies I have helped care for that were put into a routine from the very early days have ever suffered from nightmares, which leads me to believe that a consistent routine is as essential for older children as for babies.

The following will help give you a clearer understanding of nightmares and their possible causes, as well as offering some guidelines for dealing with them:

- Nightmares occur during the second half of the night, when a child is in an REM sleep cycle, often referred to as the light sleep. The child will cry out during the nightmare, and once awake may take some time to return to sleep if he cannot be convinced there is nothing to be frightened about.

- Go to your child immediately to calm and reassure him. If he is old enough to explain his nightmare and wants to talk about it, listen sympathetically but do not force him to give details. Try to use the same calm approach and soothing words each time. Once he has calmed down, tuck him up with a favourite toy and remind him you are just next-door. If he says he is frightened of the dark, it is advisable to plug in one of the very low voltage socket lights for reassurance.

- During the third year, the physical, mental and emotional demands on a child increase very rapidly. In order to cope with these, it is essential that he have a consistent bedtime routine at a regular time. I believe that children under three years of age can rarely cope with a bedtime any later than 7.30pm, especially once they are attending nursery school or have dropped their midday nap. In my experience children who have frequent late nights are much more likely to suffer from disturbed sleep.

- Over-stimulation before bedtime nearly always ends up in tears when the parents lose their temper with a child who becomes overexcited and refuses to calm down. A child who has had to be reprimanded and goes to bed fretful will be much more likely to wake in the night. Keep things as calm and quiet as possible after the bath. Discourage your child from running around and avoid any rough and tumble games.

- The majority of children under three years of age do not have a clear understanding of the difference between reality and fantasy, and the wrong type of bedtime story or video can be the cause of nightmares. Try to avoid stories and videos that involve violence. For example, stories like *Little Red Riding Hood* and *The Three Little Pigs* could certainly cause nightmares for a child with a vivid imagination. With a second or third child it may be necessary to stagger the bedtimes so he is not subjected to stories and videos that are not suitable for his age.

- A child who has been used to his mother's undivided attention can feel threatened if the arrival of a new baby results in a sudden change in his daily routine. It is important to try to organise the baby's feeding and sleeping so you have time to give your toddler some undivided attention at certain times throughout the day. By making sure the baby is settled in bed at 6.30pm you will have time to give your older child the extra reassurance he needs at bedtime.

- If your child starts to wake up regularly from nightmares it is worth keeping a diary of his daily activities, in particular writing down anything that appears to trigger anxiety or upset him. It is also worthwhile writing down the details of the nightmare. Sometimes a pattern emerges which links the daytime activities to the nightmare and pinpoints the cause. For example, a child who is frightened of dogs may be prone to nightmares when he comes into contact with one. Likewise, feeling intimidated by an aggressive child at playgroup may also be a trigger for disturbed sleep.

- If the nightmares become more frequent and continue for more than a few weeks it is advisable to ask your doctor for a referral to a sleep clinic.

Sophie, aged 35 months

Sophie had slept through the night consistently since she was nine weeks old, apart from a few occasions when she was unwell. She was nearly three years old when her brother was born, and it was about a month later that she started to have nightmares. She would wake up screaming every night, usually between 3am and

5am. Both parents would go immediately to reassure her the minute she started screaming, although it could take over an hour before they could get her to calm down. The nightmare was always the same – a big tiger was trying to get in the window. The more her parents tried to convince her that the tiger was in her dream, the more hysterical and adamant she became that the tiger was outside and trying to get to her.

The situation got worse when Sophie's screaming started to cause the baby to wake up for a second time in the night. Normally he would wake up around 2.30am, feed quickly and settle back to sleep around 3.15am until 6.30am. He now had to be settled back to sleep again around 4.30–5.00am, after he was woken by Sophie's crying.

As my booking with the family was soon coming to an end, I was desperate to sort out the situation, knowing full well that it would be extremely tough on the parents if they had to attend to both the baby and Sophie in the night. I was also concerned that the exhaustion of dealing with Sophie in the night was causing a drop in her mother's milk supply. I suggested that I take Sophie's monitor for a couple of nights to give her mother a rest.

The first night Sophie woke up screaming at 4.30am. I went straight to her to reassure her. I decided against trying to convince her there wasn't a tiger, as I had noticed that when her parents took this approach it only seemed to make her more hysterical. Instead, I got her out of bed and took her to the window and asked her to show me where the tiger was. She pointed down to the bottom of the garden and said he was hiding behind the shed. I agreed with her that there was something there, but I was sure it was a big stripy kitten and not a tiger. I explained that his mummy had specially chosen to leave him in our garden, as she knew we would look after him while she went hunting for food. The growling noise she heard at the window was not actually a tiger but the kitten asking for a drink of milk.

Within minutes of my telling Sophie this story she had calmed down, and within 10 minutes of my tucking her up in bed she was fast asleep.

The following morning Sophie remembered everything we had talked about in the night and was keen to go looking for the kitten at the bottom of the garden. I explained that the kitten only visited at night when his mother went hunting, but we could go *down to the shed and leave him a bowl of milk for his return that night. That night Sophie again woke up at 4am screaming, but settled within minutes of me reassuring her that the noise she heard was only the kitten shouting 'thank you' for his milk.*

From then on the imaginary kitten became a real part of Sophie's life, and every evening she would put a bowl of milk out for him. The wakings in the night became fewer and fewer, and when reminded that it was Tiger the kitten growling for his milk and not the fierce tiger, she would settle back to sleep within minutes. Within a couple of weeks the nightmares had stopped, although Sophie continued to put out the bowl of milk at night for the kitten for a further five months. Then one evening as her mother was pouring out the milk, Sophie announced, 'Mummy, you only have to put pretend milk in the bowl. Tiger's a pretend kitten not a real one!'

Night terrors

Night terrors are much rarer than nightmares, and a child having a night terror will behave very differently from a child who is having a nightmare. It can be very frightening for parents the first time they witness their child having a night terror. Most parents find their child sitting bolt upright in bed screaming, eyes wide open and staring straight ahead as if witnessing something really horrific. Sometimes the screaming is accompanied by incoherent moaning and thrashing around, causing the child to sweat so profusely that they appear to have a fever. Unlike the child who wakes up screaming after a nightmare and looks for comfort and reassurance, a screaming child having a night terror cannot be comforted. Although his eyes are wide open, most experts are in agreement that the child is still most definitely asleep, and parents are advised to resist waking him.

The following are suggestions on how to deal with your child if he is suffering from night terrors:

• Night terrors occur during the non-REM sleep, often referred to as the very deep sleep, usually within one to four hours of falling asleep. Night terrors usually last between 10 and 20 minutes, and provided the child is not woken up, he will settle back to sleep quickly once the terror is over.

- A child having a night terror is rarely aware of his parents' presence. Trying to calm your child down by cuddling him during a terror will probably make things worse. Unless he shows signs of wanting to be held, it is better to just stay close by so that if needed you can prevent him from injuring himself.

- As the terror is coming to an end, your child will begin to calm down and relax; at this stage you can help to settle him down by tucking him in. Try to avoid waking him or, if he does wake, avoid asking him whether he has had a bad dream. In the morning it is better not to mention the terror, as your child may get very upset being questioned about something of which he has no recollection.

- Dr Richard Ferber believes that with very young children the cause of night terrors is overtiredness. He advises that parents should ensure their child gets sufficient sleep, and if necessary consider an earlier bedtime. He also emphasises the importance of a regular and consistent daytime routine.

- Some experts suggest that a child suffering from frequent night terrors should be gently roused 10–15 minutes before the terror usually occurs and then settled back to sleep within five minutes. But other experts argue that this could lead to problems if a child wakes up fully and refuses to go back to sleep.

- Although most experts say that all children eventually grow out of night terrors, I think it would be advisable to discuss things with your doctor if your child is having frequent night terrors.

Nightmares and night terrors are two of the most common sleeping problems experienced by children during their third year. If dealt with properly these problems can usually be eliminated very quickly.

Potty training

'At what age should I start to potty train?' and 'How long will it take?' are questions I am frequently asked by parents. While all children are different, in my experience of working with hundreds of mothers and children, the majority are ready to be trained somewhere between the ages of 18 and 24 months. Before 18 months, very few children's muscles are developed enough for the bladder control necessary for potty training. While we have all heard the stories from our mothers, aunties and grandmas of how in their day a baby was potty trained by the age of one year, the reality is that it was really the mother who was trained and not the baby. By sitting the baby on the potty at frequent intervals during the day she would, more often than not, catch the urine or the bowel movement. While this obviously saved her the laborious task of washing and sterilising terry nappies, the baby could not be called potty trained in the true sense.

A toddler who is truly potty trained will recognise when he needs to pass urine or have a bowel movement and be capable of going to his potty, pulling down his own pants and using the potty, before pulling his pants up again.

When to start

Once your toddler reaches 18 months there are signs to watch out for that indicate he may be ready for potty training. However, I should point out that the success of potty training will depend not only on your toddler being ready but also on you being ready. All too often I hear horror stories of how potty training was a nightmare and took ages, the conclusion being that the child wasn't ready. In reality it was very often the parents who weren't ready. Even if your toddler is showing most of the signs listed opposite, it is inadvisable to begin training unless you have the time to devote yourself to the task 100 per cent. It is not something to undertake if you are about to move house or have just had a baby, or your toddler is just getting over an illness.

To train your toddler quickly and successfully, it is very important that not only are you in a relaxed state of mind, but also that any older or younger siblings are happy and in a good enough routine to allow you complete concentration and the extra time needed if you want to achieve this.

Provided you are feeling in a positive frame of mind, the time is right for the rest of the family, and your toddler is showing all of the signs listed, you should manage to train him successfully within one week.

The following signs indicate whether your toddler is ready to potty train:

- He is over 18 months of age and his nappy is frequently dry when you get him up from his lunchtime nap. A dry nappy a couple of hours after his last nappy change is also an indication that he is getting some bladder control.
- He shows signs of awareness when doing a poo; i.e. he goes very quiet and squeezes his legs together or points to his nappy and says 'poo' or 'pee pee' when he has done one.
- He can understand and follow simple instructions, for example, 'Go and fetch your ball' or 'Put your toy in the box'.
- He is eager to participate in taking off his own clothes, i.e. shoes, socks and shorts, and understands what pulling his shorts up and down means.
- He has the ability to sit still and occupy himself or concentrate for 5–10 minutes with a toy or a book.

Things needed for potty training

Before you begin to think of preparing your child for potty training make sure that you have all the right equipment.

Two potties

If you live in a home with more than one floor, it is essential to have two potties, one for upstairs and one for downstairs. This saves having to transfer them up and down stairs. Remember that during the early stages of training it is often a case of getting the potty to the child rather than the child to the potty. Potties should be of a simple, sturdy design with a wide brim and a splashguard at the front. They should also have an extra-wide base so that the potty stays on the floor when your child stands up. Avoid fancy or complicated designs with lids at this stage. It is a good idea to buy identical potties, as this prevents the scenario of a child refusing to use the blue one upstairs and insisting on needing the green one downstairs.

Child's loo seat

This is a specially designed seat that fits inside the normal loo seat. Choose one that is well padded and has handles at each side that the child can hold on to to keep himself steady.

Ten pairs of pants

It is important to buy pants a couple of sizes bigger than your child's usual size, making it easier for your child to pull them up and down by himself. This also allows for shrinkage due to washing and drying.

Selection of storybooks, cassette tapes and videos

Buy a selection of short story books and nursery rhyme tapes so your child is less likely to become bored while on the potty. Video some suitable children's programmes that can be used as a last resort if he becomes stubborn about using the potty.

Star chart

Design a brightly coloured star chart with your child's name on it and buy lots of different coloured stars in assorted sizes. When he has successfully used the potty several times in a row, give him an extra big star for being so clever.

Face cloths

It is easier for a small child to dry his hands himself on a small face cloth than on a towel. Choose several decorated with his favourite cartoon characters to encourage hand washing after using the potty.

Booster step

This is a small step for your child to stand on. It enables him to reach the basin more easily when washing his hands, and eventually it helps him to reach the loo.

Clothing

For the first few days of potty training it is better for you to dress your child in a very short tee shirt that does not need to be pulled up above the pants. However, once the training is under way and going well make sure you dress him in clothes that he finds quick and easy to handle when he uses the potty. For example, vests that fasten between the legs should be changed to ordinary ones. Also avoid dungarees and trousers with lots of buttons and belts. Until he is trained it is better to go for simple shorts or tracksuit type bottoms with a tee shirt or sweatshirt.

Preparation for training: Stage one

If your toddler is nearing 18 months there are many things that you can do to help prepare him for potty training. As all children of this age love to role-play, the first step is to take him to the bathroom with you as often as possible. At this stage do not remove his nappy but do encourage him to sit on his potty and watch you as you demonstrate and describe what you are doing. This will go a long way towards teaching your child in advance what will eventually be expected of him. The important thing at this stage is that he learns to sit still on the potty while you explain what you are doing using clear simple language. The following example illustrates the main points you want to get across to your child:

- 'Mummy needs to go and do a pee pee.' Helpful action: take his hand and lead him to the bathroom.
- 'Mummy does pee pee in the loo.' Helpful action: show him the loo, pointing to where the pee pee goes.
- 'Mummy is pulling down her pants.' Helpful action: demonstrate how you pull your pants down.
- 'Mummy is going to sit down on the loo and do pee pee, and James can sit on his potty.' Helpful action: applaud when he sits on his potty and praise him by saying: 'James is such a clever boy sitting so still on his potty.'
- 'Mummy has finished pee pee and she's going to pull up her nice dry pants.' Helpful action: demonstrate how you pull your pants up.

Finally, when you wash your hands encourage him to join in, washing and drying his own hands at the same time as you are doing yours. Place a lot of emphasis on the words 'wet' and 'dry', demonstrating how his hands become wet with water when washed, then dry when wiped with the towel. Occasionally, it is a good idea deliberately to wet the hand towel; allow him to feel the wet towel as you explain how much nicer it is to dry his hands on a clean dry towel. He should then be allowed to choose between the wet and the dry towel, for drying hands. This will help him to understand the difference between wet and dry.

When he shows signs of trying to copy you and participate in the above procedures, provided he is also showing some of the other signs of readiness for potty training, he should be encouraged to sit on his potty without his nappy while you prepare the bath. A time limit of 5–10 minutes is long enough, and if he manages to do anything in the potty remember to give lots of praise. When praising your child it is important that he understands why you are pleased with him. For example it is better to say how clever he is at sitting on his potty, or how clever he is at peeing in his potty than to say what a good boy he is, as he may start to think he is bad if he doesn't manage to make it to the potty.

Once he is happy to sit on the potty at bath time, you should try sitting him on it after breakfast and when you get him up from his nap. If he has been happy sitting on his potty at the above times for at least a week, you can seriously consider putting him in pants and training him to use the potty during the day. *However, as I keep stressing, the success of potty training will depend not only on your child being ready, but also on you being ready.*

Clean before dry

Many children are clean before they are dry, as it is easier for them to control their bowels than their bladder. If your child does a poo around the same time every day, it is worthwhile sitting him on the potty at that time as well as the times mentioned above. It can be a bit hit and miss at this stage: sometimes a child will do a poo in the potty, other times he will do it the minute he puts his nappy on. If this happens, do not make a fuss; simply change his nappy and tell him that the next time he needs a poo he should try to do it in his potty. The important thing is not to show disapproval or to scold the child if he doesn't manage to poo in the potty every time. Encouragement and gentle reassurance will, in the long term, get better results.

How to train: Stage two

If you have spent a minimum of two weeks following the procedures laid out in the preparation section and your child shows most of the signs of readiness listed earlier, you should be able to train your child successfully in one week. It is very important to choose a week that is fairly free of activities, especially for the first couple of days, so explain to family and friends that you are potty training and will be unavailable for telephone calls and visits during the daytime. If you have other children, it is probably better to start at the weekend, when your husband can help out.

Your toddler will need your constant attention and encouragement during the first couple of days, otherwise he will very quickly lose interest.

Day one

On the first day of training, once your toddler has had his breakfast he should be put straight into his 'special big boy pants'. If you have followed the steps listed in the preparation stage he will already have some idea of what it is he is expected to do, so keep explanations and instructions as clear and simple as possible. Explain simply that he is a big boy now and can wear pants like Mummy and Daddy, and that he can use his potty when he needs to do a pee pee or a poo. Also continue taking him with you to the bathroom and explaining what you are doing. Suggest he sits on his potty at the same time so that you can both do a pee pee.

During the first couple of days he will need frequent reminders to sit on the potty; therefore it is better to try and contain the training to one room. If you have to move between two rooms, make sure that you are prepared and have a selection of books ready in each room. It is very important that should you need to go to the other room for even a few minutes, you take the toddler and the potty.

He should be encouraged to sit on the potty every 15 minutes from when he last finished, ideally for a period of 5–10 minutes each time. Some children are happy to sit longer and others get bored very quickly. If your child is one of the latter, encourage him to look at a book or sing along to a cassette tape. Once he has successfully used the potty several times, the length of time between reminders can be gradually extended. The length of time it takes for a child to use the potty several times successfully varies from child to child. Some of the children I have trained pee regularly in the potty within a couple of hours, but with others it can take several hours. Do not despair if your child wets his pants quite a few times before he manages to do it in the potty. Once he does manage to pee in it a couple of times in a row, he will be so proud of himself that he will be very keen to keep showing you his new skill.

The important thing is not to make a big fuss or show displeasure when he does have an accident. Change his pants and continue to be enthusiastic about his big boy pants and how clever he is at sitting on his potty. When he is successful at using the potty, tell him how clever he is at peeing in the potty and how happy and proud Daddy will be. Lots of praise, hugs and applause, along with the use of a star chart, is the most effective way of encouraging him to continue using the potty. All children respond better to encouragement and praise than to criticism, and also the star chart will be a visible reminder of how clever he is at using the potty.

I have found it very useful to keep a second chart detailing the progress of potty training. It is a great help to see a pattern emerging of how often your toddler needs to urinate and whether successful use of the potty was self-motivated or not. Draw a simple chart like the one opposite. Record the time he urinates and tick the appropriate column. In the potty column, use one tick when he urinates in the potty after being instructed by you, and two ticks when he urinates in the potty of his own accord.

By the end of the first day, there should be more ticks in the potty column than in the accident column. If your child has no ticks in the potty column, it is clear that, for whatever reason, he is not ready to be potty trained and it would be better to go back to the preparation stage for a further week or two.

However, if your child has shown all the signs of readiness and you have followed all the preparation instructions laid out in Stage one, he will probably have at least two or three ticks in the potty column.

Potty Progress Chart

Time	Potty	Accident	Comments

At the end of the first day, regardless of how successful your child was at using his potty, it is important to tell him how proud you are of him for being so clever at using his potty. No reference should be made to any accidents that have occurred during the day. Also, get him to choose the pants he will wear the following day. This helps to reinforce the idea of wearing them.

To help avoid boredom setting in during the second day of training, try to arrange for one of your toddler's friends to come round for a short play date. This can be used as a further encouragement to your child; i.e. 'Tommy will be so excited to see you in your big boy pants when he visits tomorrow.' It is even better if the friend is potty trained or being potty trained.

Day two
By the second day of training, your chart should begin to show a pattern of more regular intervals between the times your child needs to pass urine. This pattern will serve as a guide as to how often you need to remind him and how often he is using the potty of his own accord. Obviously, the aim is for him to need fewer and fewer reminders from you and for there to be fewer and fewer accidents. For this to happen it is important that the potty is still kept within full view and within easy reach.

As the day progresses, you should gradually go from reminding him to sit on the potty to asking him if he needs to use the potty. It is important for his mental and physical awareness that you start to allow him some of the responsibility of deciding when he needs to use the potty, even if it means occasional accidents. Accidents will be more likely to happen if your child is playing and forgets or if he gets excited.

Day three

By the third day, a definite pattern should have emerged regarding how often he needs to use the potty. The progress chart should be of help when planning the best time for your first outing. Ideally, it should be a short visit to one of his friends who lives close by. Before leaving the house your toddler should be encouraged to use the potty so as to avoid any accidents on the journey. Do not be tempted to put him back into a nappy or disposable pull-up trainer pants on outings, as this will only give confusing signals, and is one of the main reasons why potty training can take so long.

Consistency is of the utmost importance if you want to potty train quickly and successfully. Dress your toddler in pants at all times during the day – nappies are for sleep times only. While there may be a few accidents during the first few days, these mishaps will actually help your child to become more aware of his need to urinate and the difference between wet and dry. It is best not to make a fuss or scold your toddler if he has an accident, simply remind him what the potty is for.

In the early days it is advisable to take a couple of spare changes of clothes and pants on outings and a plastic bag to put them in if they get wet. Until your toddler gets used to using the lavatory you will also need to take his potty. Although I have never used one for a toddler, there are special portable potties now available for travelling.

Until your toddler is properly trained it is advisable to take precautions when travelling in the car or using the buggy. I would advise buying a thin cushion pad and covering it with a polythene bag. This can then be covered with a removable, washable, decorative cover. It can be your child's special cushion and be used in the buggy, on the car seat or when visiting friends, and is safer than just placing a plastic bag on the seat. I have found that when a plastic bag is placed on a seat, the child often sees it as a safety net and is less inclined to mention that he needs to pee. He is unaware that his cushion has a plastic cover, and because it is his special cushion he will be more likely to want to keep it dry.

Days four to seven

By the fourth day, the majority of toddlers are regularly using their potty without prompting, with just the occasional accident occurring. Over the next few days the potty should gradually be moved nearer and nearer to the bathroom. Once your toddler shows signs that he can control his bladder long enough to get to the bathroom, it should remain there permanently. If a couple of hours have gone by without him using the potty and he seems particularly engrossed in something, it would be a good idea to remind him where the potty is.

By the end of the first week, the majority of toddlers are dry most of the time, with only the occasional accident. To ensure continued success it is important that you never put your toddler back in nappies apart from sleep times. This only confuses the toddler and is one of the main reasons potty training can become a problem and take many months to crack.

Sleep times

I would continue to put a toddler in nappies during his daytime sleep until his nappy has been consistently dry for at least two weeks when he gets up. After that I would feel confident that it was safe to abandon them. For the night-time sleep, I would continue with nappies for several months. It is my experience that very few children are capable of going through the night before the age of three years, and with boys it may be even later.

I have found that parents who push night-time training before this age often end up with other problems. One major one is that once the nappy is abandoned it is usually necessary either to install a night-light or to leave the door slightly ajar. With toddlers under three years the temptation to start running around in the middle of the night is often too hard to resist, especially if they know Mummy is attending to a younger sibling. With a child over three years who is consistently dry and clean, I would explain to him that he no longer needs to wear a nappy at night, and make sure that he goes on the potty just before he gets into bed. Once your child stops wearing a nappy at night it is important to make sure that the last drink is given at least an hour before bedtime.

Bedwetting
It is fairly common for young children to have an occasional accident at night. However, it can be a real problem if bedwetting

becomes a regular occurrence. The broken nights' sleep and changing of wet sheets can be exhausting for parents and lead to the child feeling anxious and guilty. If your child has been dry for many weeks and suddenly starts wetting the bed, a visit to the doctor should be considered to rule out the possibility of a urinary infection. Many experts suggest that a relapse may also be caused by emotional problems, but in my experience this is rarely the case. The majority of parents I have worked with believe that excessive amounts of fluid prior to bedtime can be a major cause of bedwetting; therefore they allow no drinks after 6pm.

If a child under four years who has been dry only for a few weeks then starts to wet the bed regularly, it is probably because he isn't quite ready to last through the night. It may be preferable to put him back in nappies for a short while to avoid bedwetting becoming an issue.

If your child is over four years of age and, despite restricting fluids, you are getting a wet bed every morning, it may be worthwhile lifting him and putting him on the potty at your bedtime.

Lifting at 10pm
Years ago, childcare experts advised parents to lift their baby at 10pm and put him on the potty to pass urine. These experts believed that the age at which a child gains bladder control at night depends largely on the mother's skill in training him in infancy.

The childcare manuals written in the 1930s and 1940s stressed that lifting should be a habit that is formed in infancy. Mothers were advised that regularly lifting the child every night until he was four years old was key to teaching him how to stay dry throughout the night. If their laziness prevented them from doing this, they would create a habit difficult to cure; a child who got used to waking up with a wet nappy would quickly begin to believe that it was normal.

While many parents do still lift their children at their bedtime, the majority of childcare experts today are against this practice. They believe that this approach only conditions the child to pass urine at certain times. I would tend to agree with this, and would only consider lifting a child if he was over four years of age and despite monitoring fluids in the evening, the bed was wet every morning.

A nanny friend and I successfully used the lifting approach as a last resort when working in the Middle East with a family of serious bedwetters. The six children aged from four to 14 years were taken very sleepily at different times to the loo in the late evening. Occasionally, one or the other would wake up wet, but much to the relief of the laundry staff, most mornings the beds were dry.

If you decide to try this approach, it is important that the child is kept sleepy and not stimulated. The lights should be kept very dim, and talking, if any, should be minimised. Children under three years could be put on the potty instead of being taken to the bathroom. Some experts claim that varying the time of lifting will help reduce the possibility of conditioning the child to need to urinate at the same time every night.

If you find that lifting your child is working, it is worthwhile using a star chart. On the mornings when the bed is dry he gets a star; three stars and he gets a special treat – perhaps an ice cream.

If the bedwetting improves, I would advise telling your child that he is a big boy now and doesn't need lifting any more in the night. Suggest to him that if he does wake in the night and needs a pee he should call for you to come and help him. Although it will mean you getting up in the night for a short while, I usually find that as the child's confidence increases, he will be persuaded to use the potty by himself.

Again, I have found that, if used properly, the star chart is very effective during these various stages.

The stubborn child

Occasionally, I have a child who refuses to go on the potty. If he is under two-and-a-half years, I do not force the issue. However, with a child nearer three years of age I would probably resort to bribery. I know the majority of experts frown upon this advice, but sometimes, especially with a very stubborn child, it is the only way.

While a child over three years may not show all the signs necessary for potty training, he is usually capable of being trained. I would skip the preparation stage and go straight into potty training, using a star chart. I would explain that every time he does a pee in the potty he will get a star – and for every star he will get a treat. The treat can be a raisin or a very small sweet such as a smartie. Believe me, it does work, provided of course that the child receives no other treats throughout the day. I generally find that within two days the child is regularly asking for the potty, then the star, followed by the treat.

Once I see a regular pattern emerging I explain to the child that I have run out of the treats. I suggest that the next three pees in the potty would deserve a trip to the shop for a special ice cream. By using the delaying tactic of a bigger treat for more pees in the potty, I eventually arrive at a stage where the child uses the potty throughout the day and ends up with only one treat in the evening.

Hygiene

During the early stages of potty training you will need to wipe your toddler's bottom and help him wash and dry his hands. By the time most children get to three years, they are becoming more independent and insist on doing these things for themselves. It is important to help them practise how to wipe their bottom properly (girls from front to back) and how to wash their hands thoroughly. The use of novelty soaps and hand towels with cartoons on them can help make hand washing and drying more fun. It is essential to teach your child the importance of proper hygiene.

Regression

All toddlers and children will continue to have the occasional accident once they are potty trained. The important thing is to stay calm and consistent and not be tempted to put your child back into nappies if you have a couple of bad days. Occasionally, a toddler or child who has been dry for many months may regress completely. This often happens around the time when a new brother or sister arrives, when he starts playgroup or when there is a similar emotional upheaval. If your child suddenly regresses and appears to be more withdrawn or is more demanding and displaying unusual aggressive behaviour, the regression is probably psychological. If his behaviour is normal, it may be worth a visit to the doctor to rule out the possibility of a urine infection.

Whatever has caused the regression, I would not advise going back to nappies. Although this may mean many wet pants for a short spell, being patient, consistent and encouraging will eventually get your child back on track. It is also worthwhile doing a progress chart for a couple of days again, to establish how often the accidents are happening (see page 83). A pattern usually emerges regarding how often he has an accident, and this will enable you to remind him to use the potty at these regular intervals. If he is reluctant to use the potty, take him with you when you need to go to the loo yourself. Making a game of using the loo at the same time will often encourage a toddler to go on the potty while you are using the loo. Obviously, this plan is more likely to be successful if followed at roughly the times you think he may need to pee.

Reintroducing a line on his star chart for successful use of the potty can also be an incentive.

3

The Power of Play

All parents want their children to grow up to be popular and well liked. A child who has learned to compromise, play fairly and be considerate of the needs of others will be much more likely to achieve this than a child who thinks only of his own needs and refuses to share. Play is a very important tool and can also teach children to appreciate the environment in which they are growing up.

Children use play to assimilate experiences and to develop the skills they need for interaction and communication. I believe that maximising play times in a structured and stimulating environment is one the most important aspects of developing happy and well-rounded children, capable of using their own imagination, establishing strong friendships and enjoying their siblings. A child who enjoys his own company and the company of other children at play promises to be a considerate and resourceful adult. No aspect of childcare is more important.

Arranging short play dates with one or two other children will help to prepare your child for socialising with other children. Once your toddler is happy to play alongside a couple of other toddlers you can begin to expand his circle of friends and attend activities and play dates with larger numbers of toddlers and children. However, a word of warning: some of these larger organised activities can be very competitive, with mothers boasting about how advanced their toddler is at certain skills.

Please do not fall into the trap of comparing your toddler's skills with those of other toddlers of the same age. All children develop at different rates, and the fact that some toddlers of the same age may have a larger vocabulary or can succeed at different skills better than others does not mean that they are going to be more intelligent in the long term. Over the years it has been fascinating watching many of the babies I helped care for grow. It is interesting that some of the ones who were more reserved, often very slow to talk and walk, are now turning out to be the brightest and most charming.

The important thing at this stage is not how quickly your toddler learns something but whether he enjoys learning. He should be given the opportunity to do so in a stimulating but happy and relaxed environment.

Learning from play

Playing with other children is how your toddler learns to communicate and cooperate, building up his social skills. Up to the age of two years toddlers tend to spend much of their time playing alongside each other, not with each other. During this stage of development it is important to ensure that your toddler has regular opportunities to meet other toddlers and older children, so that he begins to learn about sharing and taking turns. Your toddler will learn much by just watching and listening at this stage. By the time he reaches two years his physical and verbal skills will be more developed, giving him the confidence to start joining in games and activities with other children. A toddler who has advanced physically and mentally but not been given the opportunity to observe how other children play during the second year may well be apprehensive about joining in with others.

Types of play

Different types of play will enhance and develop your toddler's mental, physical and emotional social skills in different ways. Your toddler is an individual and will develop his own preferences for what he enjoys doing. While it is important to introduce him to lots of different activities, it is pointless to keep forcing him to do something he doesn't enjoy. I remember one mother of a 15-month-old boy who was so desperate to develop his creative skills that every afternoon she forced him to sit and paste, stick, draw or paint. Each day it would end up in tears and tantrums, with water being spilt or paint brushes being hurled across the room. I eventually persuaded her to put aside creative play for a couple of weeks and concentrate on the things he really did enjoy. When she re-introduced creative play a few weeks later, she did so no more than twice a week. He is now nearly eight years of age and proving to be a really talented little artist. Remember, more doesn't always equal better. While repetition plays an important part in helping your toddler learn something, I believe that how much a toddler enjoys doing something enhances his development as much as how often he does it.

More doesn't always equal better also goes for toys. In my experience, toddlers who have too many toys are much more likely to become bored easily and less likely to use their imagination when playing with their toys.

The following sections describe different types of play and activities that most toddlers enjoy and that will also help develop different skills.

Physical play

Physical activity is essential for a young child's health. It helps to build strong muscles, increase stamina and appetite, use up energy and, hopefully, induce sound sleep at night. It also is important during the second year for helping to develop a child's major motor body skills, which include walking, running, jumping and climbing. As your toddler becomes steadier on his feet, involving him in physical games will improve his balance and coordination. I believe that physical play is also important in helping to develop much needed social skills for later life. A toddler who learns the art of combining physical and mental coordination through activities and play in his formative years will be much more likely to have the confidence to enjoy sporting and social activities such as swimming, tennis, skiing and horse riding in later life.

During the second year your toddler should be introduced to play and activities that help him learn to run, jump, climb, walk up and down stairs, throw and kick a ball and do simple little dance steps. Some of these physical activities can also be used to help your toddler understand the concept of numbers and spatial awareness. Some toddlers are naturally more athletic than others, and the aim of physical play should be that your child has fun while learning different skills.

During the third year a child who has enjoyed and been

involved in lots of different physical activities during his second year will be much more confident about running and jumping and will have a better understanding of distance, height, etc. He will also have a better mental understanding of how games are played and be eager to join in activities that involve throwing, catching and kicking. By the time he reaches three years of age he will probably be confident about using a climbing frame or slide unaided, jumping into the swimming pool and perhaps even swimming a short length, riding a tricycle and so on.

Reading

Reading to your toddler is not only an excellent way of helping to improve his speech development but it also teaches him about the world around him and develops his imagination and concentration. Start off with simple books that show pictures of things he is familiar with. Encourage him to point to the object as you name it asking, 'Where's the dog?' 'Where's the cat?', etc. When teaching him a new word it is very important that you speak very clearly and slowly and that he is close enough to observe your mouth movements. Lift the flap and touchy-feely books are very popular with toddlers and they are an excellent way of stimulating their imagination and improving their memory.

Picture dictionaries, where you point to and name familiar objects used in everyday life, are also great for helping to develop language skills. Between 18 months and two years most toddlers will enjoy short simple stories. Choose books with one or two lines to each page. Nursery rhyme books with actions your toddler can join in with are also great fun at this age and great for improving his memory, as he will eventually start to remember where certain words come in the rhyme and join in with the word and the action.

Creative play

Creative play, using paints, crayons, playdough, etc., teaches a toddler about colour, shape and texture and helps to develop his imagination and hand–eye coordination skills, as well as improving his concentration. During the second year introduce your toddler to finger painting and blob painting using special thickened finger paint, then progress to painting pictures using simple blocks or sponges, then chunky paintbrushes. Once he is more competent at holding a paintbrush, his paintings will take the form of different brush strokes as opposed to blobs. During the third year his painting will become more structured and he may be able to paint something that resembles a house, flower or person.

Chunky first crayons are your toddler's first step towards learning to write and draw. In the beginning his writing will take the form of side-to-side scribbles, but as his grip and hand control develop, along with his hand–eye coordination, his scribbling will start to include more circular shapes. By the time he is entering his third year his coordination skills should have developed sufficiently for him to be capable of using less chunky crayons. He will be able to draw simple shapes and colour them in using colouring pencils. By four years of age his drawings will become more recognisable as familiar objects and people in his life.

Your toddler will love the feel of playdough but during his second year he will probably be happy just to pull it or squash and squeeze it. Shape cutters can be used to help him understand the concept of different shapes and sizes. As his imagination and coordination skills improve during his third year, he will start forming shapes independently, which will eventually begin to resemble familiar objects.

Fantasy play

Fantasy play helps to develop your toddler's imagination and is also a way of enabling him to express his thoughts and emotions. During the second year your toddler will use his soft toys and replica toys of adult equipment to create pretend games. Teddies and dolls will be bathed and fed and taken for imaginary walks in toy prams or buggies. When visitors come to the house he will expect them also to participate in imaginary tea parties. As your toddler's imagination develops, he will use pretend play as a way of expressing emotions. If he is feeling angry or frustrated, one teddy may suddenly get a smack or not be allowed a pretend drink, while another teddy may get hugs and kisses.

During the third year your child will use dressing up and lots of role-play to create more complex games involving his friends to help act out favourite characters from books or videos or people and situations he remembers. Role-play is also an excellent way for children to use their imagination to control situations and learn how to solve problems.

Problem-solving play

Jigsaws, shape-sorters, matching games, Duplo and Lego are all toys that stimulate mental development by encouraging your child to think about ways of solving problems. They will also help improve his concentration and hand–eye coordination. Toddlers can get very frustrated when trying to match things up, but trying to work out what goes where and what matches what is all part of the learning process. Teaching him about the process of elimination will help reduce his frustration without you solving the problem for him.

Social play

As your toddler heads towards the end of his second year various signs may indicate that he is getting ready to develop real friendships and play *with* other children as opposed to alongside them. The most obvious of these is his ability to string several words together to express his thoughts, feelings and needs more easily. His major and minor motor skills will have improved dramatically. He will be much more confident about games that involve running, jumping and catching.

Social play with children his own age will teach your toddler good communication skills, how to share with other children and how to cooperate so that he can enjoy playing in group situations. By arranging short play dates with other children his own age and taking him to small playgroups you will help prepare him for the time when he will be ready to form friendships. Use his soft toys during role-play to help develop a sense of caring, for example, 'Teddy is so happy when you share your juice', 'Dolly loves it when you cuddle her so gently'. Reading him books and allowing him to watch videos that involve kind and caring gestures will also encourage caring behaviour. Play sharing games with your child and praise him when he shares things without being prompted by you. Adding a line to his star chart and giving him a star when he is particularly considerate of others will help to reinforce caring behaviour.

Playing fairly

Sharing is something that all children have to learn, and the best way to achieve this is to ensure that your child has regular opportunities to play with other children. Up to the age of two years children tend to spend much of their time playing alongside each other, not with each other. It is only during the third year that they begin to show signs of participating in play with other children. During this stage of development arranging short play dates with only one or two other children will make it easier for you to teach your child about sharing and taking turns. It is also easier to control things when there are fewer children, therefore avoiding tears and tantrums. Choose friends carefully, avoiding children who are aggressive and unruly. Sometimes it can be a good thing to invite a child who is slightly older and has learnt the importance of give and take while playing.

Prepare your child in advance by talking about getting out the toys he thinks his friends would like to play with. If during the play date your child gets possessive about a particular toy another child is playing with, do not force him to give the toy back to the child. Instead take the other child aside and find him something special to play with. Young children hate being ignored and you will find that this way your child is much more likely to offer to give the toy back than if you try to force him to do so. When it comes to snack time encourage your child to offer the biscuits to his guests first, and remember always to express your pleasure and approval when he shows consideration towards others. A star on his star chart on the days he has played nicely with his friends will also go a long way towards encouraging good behaviour.

Television and video

When used selectively, I think a certain amount of television or video watching can help stimulate a young child's natural curiosity, develop his imagination and improve his vocabulary.

However, there has been lots of research to suggest that excessive TV or video watching has the opposite effect, seriously hampering language acquisition and social skills and causing physical unfitness in childhood and later life. Cartoons containing violence can cause copycat behaviour, and I have certainly observed a link between aggressive behaviour and TV watching. The toddlers and young children of families that I have worked with who were allowed to watch cartoons and videos two or three times a day, were definitely more prone to temper tantrums and aggressive outbursts than those whose screen viewing was both restricted and selected for suitability.

The following guidelines will help ensure that your child benefits from what he does watch and doesn't become a TV addict:

- Be selective about the times of day that your child is allowed to watch TV and the number of times he watches. In my opinion, once or twice a day for a short spell of 20 minutes or so is more than enough for children under four years of age. Watching TV or a video for a short spell can be used to help your toddler relax once he drops his midday nap and gives you time to recharge your batteries after a hectic morning.
- Whenever possible, try to sit with your child while he is watching a TV programme or video so that you can discuss what is happening. If a cartoon character is doing something naughty or violent, you can explain why he shouldn't have done it.
- Be selective about what you allow your child to watch. Excessive viewing of cartoons, which often contain violence without consequence, will do little to enhance his development or his behaviour.
- Try to pre-record TV programmes so that you can fast forward adverts that expose your child to excessive promotion of sweets and toys.

Setting the pace

During the second year your toddler develops a real sense of self. As his walking and talking skills develop, he will become more independent, and his personality will begin to shine through. Life with a child of this age can be likened to a trip on a rollercoaster, as your toddler begins to realise that how he behaves will influence how others treat him. Trying to keep a toddler of this age occupied and happy can be both exhilarating and exhausting for parents. This is probably the most frustrating time of a young child's life, as he struggles to achieve many physical tasks and is not yet articulate enough to express his feelings and emotional needs. During this stage of rapid development, play and social activities are an important factor in helping him learn how to walk, talk and socialise with other toddlers.

While play and activities are essential for stimulating the minds of young children and helping them to develop these different skills, it is equally important that their day is structured to include quiet times when they can relax and reflect about what they have been doing. Many childcare experts now believe that parents who fill their child's every waking hour with constant stimulation and activities are putting him at risk of 'toddler burnout', not allowing enough time for him to recharge his batteries.

In my experience, toddlers aged between one and two-and-a-half are most at risk, because they are at a stage of learning many different physical and mental skills at the same time.

All children must be allowed to develop at their own pace and all children need to have a balance between calm quiet times during the day and times filled with different activities. When planning your toddler's day try to balance out play dates and activities so that part of each day is quiet time and every other day involves time for play in which the child has to use his own imagination to amuse himself. Toddlers and children who have too many toys and are constantly entertained and stimulated soon become hyperactive, demanding more and more attention because they get bored very quickly.

It is also important to encourage toddlers and young children to play independently for short spells and not to entertain them constantly. If your toddler has got used to having your undivided attention all the time, start off by leaving him alone with his toys for three to four minutes before joining him. Gradually build up the time between leaving him to play and you playing with him until he is happy to play for 15–20 minutes on his own.

4
Mother Care, Other Care

It is quite natural and normal for childcare to be shared with other people. Since the beginning of time, parenting has been undertaken within a community and usually within a family. Children could expect to be cared for by a wide circle of people including grandparents, aunts and uncles, cousins. It is only recently, with families living further apart from each other and close-knit communities breaking down, that mothers have been expected to go it alone. There are good reasons for finding help and support with childcare, not only for your toddler's growth and development but also for your own. It may also be necessary for the simple reason that you have to return to work and need someone to care for your child during the working day, whether you work part- or full-time.

If you are lucky enough to have your family living close by, your baby or toddler is probably already used to being cared for by someone other than you and your partner. If this is not the case though, it would be worthwhile considering getting your toddler used to being cared for on a regular basis by someone else, even if you don't intend to return to work. This will give you a much-deserved break during the second year, which can be very exhausting as your toddler becomes physically and mentally more demanding. If you are planning a second baby in the next year or so, it will be a great advantage to have your toddler happy to be left with someone else for a few hours a week.

I have found that parents who establish regular spells away from their toddlers are usually much more patient and tolerant of the inevitable misbehaviour that happens during the second year than those who devote themselves 24/7 to their children. Do not feel guilty about taking some time out for yourself – your life does not have to grind to a halt because you've become a mother. Spending a few hours a week doing something you enjoy, other than mothering, will not only recharge your batteries but will also help you keep things in perspective regarding your toddler's development and behaviour. Meanwhile, your child can begin to learn some independence and vital social skills.

It may be that you need to return to work after your maternity leave and will be considering childcare from early on. Today more than 60 per cent of women return to work during the nursery years, some even earlier, either on a part-time or full-time basis. This, together with the fact that family members often live far away from each other, means that many women need to consider alternative types of childcare. Women who work are sometimes made to feel guilty about it, although often they have no choice about taking paid employment for financial reasons. It is, I believe, possible to have a perfectly happy, healthy child who is accustomed to being looked after by people other than his parents. The main thing is that you make the right choice of care for your child and are confident in the abilities of the person you entrust him to.

There are three main choices when it comes to childcare. These are nanny, childminder or day nursery.

Nanny

A nanny is probably the most expensive option for child-care. Although there is talk that the government is going to provide some tax breaks for mothers who employ nannies, it will still be a costly alternative. If the nanny lives with you, there will be board and accommodation to consider, along with the payment of the nanny's tax and national insurance, her salary and any other benefits, such as being insured to drive your car. A live-out nanny will be cheaper but still expensive. The clear benefit is that your child is looked after in his own home and has the opportunity to have a strong emotional bond with one person. The structure of the day, the playtime, the companions and the nutrition of your child remain entirely in your control. A good nanny offers the best of a mother's care with the added advantage of training and perhaps a natural affinity with and enjoyment of children. She can make sure that the child has a varied and stimulating routine, with activities such as music groups, trips to the park, feeding the ducks, football in the garden or socialising with friends, and she can structure everything to suit the child.

Some people, though, are reluctant to have a stranger in their home and are not keen on the lack of accountability: a nanny has sole charge of your child and is less answerable than an official organisation. Some parents don't like to think of their child forming a strong, almost parental bond with someone who is not going to be a permanent fixture.

If you do decide to employ a nanny, the most essential thing is trust: this person will have total charge of your child and access to all areas of your life, so it is vital that you are entirely happy in your choice. You also have to like and get on with your nanny – a personality clash is going to be disastrous. Another common problem is a difference of expectation. Some parents expect the nanny to baby-sit or help with housework, and the nanny may see her hours and duties as more limited. It's important that all these things are set out clearly beforehand. Also remember that a nanny is your employee and will need a certain amount of support and appreciation. If she lives in, there will have to be respect for her own needs in terms of quiet time and a social life.

Some women choose to do a nanny share, which means that the nanny will look after two children of a similar age in one or other of the homes, which enables the mothers to share the cost. This can work very well, particularly if the mothers want to work part-time.

The following checklist will help you to select a nanny.

- If you are using a nanny agency, do not rely on them to check the personal references. It's essential that you speak to the nanny's previous employers yourself to ensure that they have been happy with their experience.
- Ask how long the candidate has worked as a nanny and why she chose this career. What are her expectations and priorities? What does she most enjoy about the job?
- Watch how she interacts with your child and how your child responds to her. A good relationship between nanny and child is essential for the success of the arrangement. Is she prepared to get down on your child's level, sitting on the floor, playing

with trains, or is she more interested in impressing her future employers?
- Does she smile readily and seem a positive person?
- How would she discipline a child? Does she believe in smacking?
- Does she have an understanding of good nutrition?
- Suggest spending an hour with her out of the house to see how she would handle a trip to the park. Is she practical and safety conscious?
- Does she enjoy child-oriented activities? Does she have a good network of professional nanny friends locally? It's nice for a toddler to socialise, but you need to ensure that this doesn't just involve nannies chatting to each other without providing enthusiasm and encouragement for your child.
- Establish a trial period to see if you are both happy with the arrangement.

Childminder

A childminder is someone who will care for your toddler in her own home. She must be registered with Ofsted (Office for Standards in Education), and her home will be inspected at least every two years to ensure that health, safety, care and education comply with their standards.

Childminders normally cost less than nannies, but as they look after more than one child, they may not be able to give your child the same one-to-one care. Childminders can care for up to six children aged under eight, of whom no more than three must be aged under five at any time. Most childminders are registered for three children under five and three children under eight at any one time. Normally, only one child may be under one year; however, a childminder may be registered to care for two children under one year where she can demonstrate that she can meet the needs of the children. The childminder's own children are taken into account and counted in these numbers. Some childminders work with an assistant and they may look after larger groups of children.

Childminders can probably offer more individual care than a day nursery, and provide more of a home-from-home experience. Their hours are usually more flexible, as each childminder organises her own time. She may well be able to accommodate your child part-time or take him to classes, playgroup or even school. It is important to remember that, unlike a day nursery, a childminder is likely to have no back-up if she is ill and to take her holidays at a different time from you.

Childminders are self-employed and therefore responsible for their own tax and national insurance contributions. Rates are normally charged on an hourly basis and costs vary depending on where you live.

The following checklist will help you to select a childminder:

- Check with the local council that the childminder you choose is registered and has satisfied inspections, and that there are no complaints on record.
- Check the childminder's qualifications and experience, and ask for the names, addresses and phone numbers of three sets of parents who can provide references.
- Always follow up references thoroughly.
- Ask how long she has worked as a childminder, why she has chosen to work as a childminder and what she enjoys most about the job.
- Watch how she interacts with your child and how your child responds to her.
- Does she or any other member of the family smoke, and do they allow visitors to smoke in the house?
- Do they keep any pets, and if so, are there litter trays inside?
- Is there a garden or a park nearby so that walks and outdoor activities are possible? Is the garden clean, tidy and safe?
- You should be allowed to view all the rooms in the house that are used for the children. Pay particular attention to the cleanliness and whether everything is childproof.
- Is there a separate bedroom with a proper cot for your toddler to have his midday nap? Will he have to share the room with other children at nap time?
- Check how many children she cares for, their ages and how many hours she looks after them. If she cares for older children before and after school, check how much time your child may have to spend sitting in a car while she drops off and picks up these children.

- Is the childminder willing to follow your instructions regarding sleeping and eating?
- Ask what sort activities she would be doing with your toddler and how she fits in the activities of any other children she is caring for. Get her to describe a typical day: how does she manage to structure feeding, rest, playing and outside activities, particularly if she is also responsible for older or younger children?
- Ask her how she would deal with tantrums, discipline, jealousy and refusal to eat or sleep. It is very important that you get her to give you her views on these issues before you give yours.
- Discuss what would happen in the event of her being ill and what happens at holiday times. If you go away on holiday, will you have to pay her in order to retain your child's place?
- Are you happy with the general atmosphere of the child-minder's home?

Day nursery

This is the most popular form of childcare. The number of day nurseries has increased dramatically in the last couple of years, and places are often hard to get at the most impressive ones. The cost varies according to the kind of nursery you choose: state or private. Many nurseries offer Government-funded, free part-time early education places for eligible four-year-olds and some three-year-olds – your local council is the best source of information for this. You may need to register very early, as places are in short supply. Most nurseries offer full-time and part-time places; the majority offer extended daycare from 8am to 6pm (referred to as wraparound care) and most are open throughout the year. Your local Children's Information Service will provide you with the details of nurseries in your area.

The best nurseries offer a wide range of interesting activities for babies and toddlers in a structured and ordered environment. There will be lots of play and supervised physical activity, with attention paid to developing skills such as speaking, listening, concentration and learning to work and play with others. There should be opportunities for younger toddlers to rest and sleep in appropriate surroundings, and healthy, fresh food should be provided.

Parents are often drawn to day nurseries because they like the security of an official, registered organisation that has more than one trained carer to look after the children. The number of staff will usually reflect the number of children who attend. There is also the added attraction of a wide range of toys and activities and lots of other children for your toddler to mix with. The most important aspect, however, is the quality of care. A headteacher or carer will have overall responsibility for this, and should ensure that there is plenty of feedback and attention to the individual needs of the children.

Day nurseries have their disadvantages too – one of the most significant is that it is harder for a child to build a bond with staff if there is a high staff turnover or not enough one-to-one time for each child. If your child needs particular attention, it is worth seeking out a smaller nursery equipped for individual needs. Another disadvantage is that the hours are set, so there is little flexibility if problems arise, and some nurseries close for half-term and school holidays, when other arrangements will need to be made.

The following checklist will help you to select a day nursery:

- Check with the council that the day nursery has been inspected recently and read the Ofsted report to ensure that this is a good organisation. Ask to see the most recent certificate.
- Speak to other parents whose children attend the nursery to see whether they are happy with the care of their children.
- Ask about staff turnover and accountability.
- Ask about staff qualifications and training.
- Observe how the carers relate to the children.
- Do the children look happy, involved, stimulated?
- If a child is unhappy, assess how this is being handled.
- Take your child with you when you go to look around to see how he likes the environment.
- Is it very noisy? Are there separate facilities where children are able to rest?
- What sort of food do they offer to the children? Is it healthy? Ask to see the kitchen.
- Is there an outdoor play area? Is it safe and secure, with appropriate toys and activities?
- Ask how the day is structured. What sort of activities are on

offer and how long do they spend on each one? How long are the lunch/snack breaks?

- Ask to check the toilet and washing facilities.
- Will the children be taken on outings and walks? This is particularly important if your child is being enrolled full-time.

5
Routines for Toddlers (12 to 36 months)

During the second year the amount of sleep a toddler needs during the day gradually reduces. It is then possible to be more relaxed about adapting and adjusting his daily routine to fit in with his increasing need for more social activities, as he will no longer be content to lie under his play-gym or sit happily in his buggy watching the world go by. His ever increasing physical mobility and mental awareness arouse his natural desire to explore the world around him. Organised play dates and classes are an ideal way of meeting many of your toddler's physical, mental and emotional needs, as well as building up a social life and network of friends for the years ahead. However, it is still important to keep a close eye on his daytime routine. Even the most contented little baby who has always slept well during the first year can suddenly develop sleep problems during the second year. Structuring your toddler's sleep is very important if you wish to avoid him becoming overtired. Overtiredness is one of the main reasons why sleep problems occur during this stage, and the main cause of overtiredness is toddlers being overloaded with too many activities. It is important to structure your toddler's social activities so that he has some days that are not so hectic.

Another very common reason for sleeping to go wrong during the second year is that parents often miss the signs that their toddler is ready to cut back on the amount of sleep he needs during the day. This can cause problems in the night. At one year most babies are still having an average of 14–15 hours of sleep a day, divided between night-time sleep and two daytime naps. However, as they enter toddlerhood the amount of sleep needed gradually reduces to an average of 13–14 hours a day, which is usually divided between night-time sleep and one daytime nap.

Watching for the signs that your toddler is ready to cut back on his sleep can help to avoid night-time sleep problems evolving.

The following points will help you decide if your toddler is ready to cut back on his daytime sleep:

- The majority of toddlers will show signs of cutting back their sleep between the ages of 15 and 18 months, although some toddlers may show signs slightly earlier than this.
- Your toddler may take longer and longer to drop off to sleep when put down for his morning nap at 9.30am, or may still settle well but cut down the amount of time he sleeps to 15–20 minutes.
- He may sleep well at the morning nap but cut right back on his lunchtime nap.
- He may take longer to settle and sleep in the evening or begin to wake up earlier in the morning.

By watching for the above signs you will be able to structure your toddler's daytime sleep to ensure that his night-time sleep is not affected.

Establishing a routine after the first year

I get many calls from parents of toddlers who have not established a routine, asking if it is too late to do this during the second year. While it is never too late, it is obviously much more difficult. These toddlers are nearly always still being breast-fed or formula-fed on demand and have learned different sleep associations. During the day the toddler will usually fall asleep only when driven around in the car or taken out in the buggy. In the evening he usually needs to be rocked or fed to sleep, and in all the cases I have to deal with, the toddler usually wakes several times a night and has to be fed or rocked back to sleep. During the first year parents usually cope with this as they hold on to the hope that once their baby gets past his first birthday and starts to walk he will use up more energy and be more willing to settle by himself in the cot. This is rarely the case. Indeed, often the toddler simply becomes overtired and fights sleep even more. Rocking a baby to sleep is exhausting but possible, but trying to rock a wriggling, boisterous, overtired toddler to sleep is virtually impossible. The first thing I advise the parents is to structure their toddler's feeding and sleep times during the day. Because their toddler has learned these sleep associations, they will still have to assist him to sleep, but regulating the time he sleeps is the first step to establishing a routine.

If your toddler has no routine and you wish to establish one, use the following guidelines to help you:

- Check this chapter for the routine appropriate for your toddler's age, and structure his daytime feeding and sleeping according to the times in the routine. At this stage you will still need to assist him to sleep using the usual methods. If it is feeding or rocking or taking him in the car, continue to do this, but at the times stated.

- From one year of age a toddler needs a minimum of 350ml (12oz) and a maximum of 600ml (20oz) of milk a day. If your toddler is drinking in excess of this it is very likely that he is not eating enough solids. This leads to a vicious circle in which he genuinely needs to feed in the night. Therefore it is important gradually to reduce the amount of milk he is taking so his intake of solids is increased. However, until his daytime sleep is regulated you should continue to use milk to settle him in the night. If you try to eliminate the night feeds before the excessive daytime milk feeds, he will probably stay awake all night screaming for food. He will then be so tired the following day that it will be very difficult to keep him awake, making it impossible to structure his daytime sleep.

- If milk feeding is being used to settle your toddler to sleep, once you see him sleeping regularly at the right times during the day according to the routine, start to reduce the amount of milk he is taking before his naps. If he is breast-fed, gradually reduce the time you put him to the breast. If he is formula-fed, reduce the amount of formula you give him or dilute the feed. It is important that you continue to feed him as usual in the night when he wakes. As mentioned earlier, at this stage it is of no benefit for him to be awake half the night.

- After several days you should see an improvement in the amount of solids he is eating. Once this happens you can start to reduce the time he is on the breast at one of his night-time wakings. If he is formula-fed you can either reduce the amount you give or dilute the milk he is taking. If you are unsure of what solids he needs at his age, refer to page 14 for guidelines.

- By gradually reducing the amount he takes at one feed in the night you will encourage him to take more at the next waking, which in turn should help to reduce the amount of times he is waking. Once he is down to one feed in the night this can also be gradually reduced, until you reach the stage where you settle him with water or a cuddle.

- Within a couple of weeks, daytime sleep should be at regular times. The amount of solids he is taking should have increased and the amount of milk taken prior to naps decreased. The number of times he is waking in the night should also have reduced. Once this has happened you should attempt to settle him in his cot awake during the day and in the evening, and without feeding or rocking him to sleep. He will most certainly cry, but hopefully for no more than 10–20 minutes. When he wakes in the night he should also be left for 10–20 minutes to settle himself back to sleep. If he takes any longer than this to settle, you will probably have to use some form of sleep training. The two most popular methods are the gradual withdrawal method and the controlled crying method. Alternatively your health visitor or GP can refer you to a sleep clinic, which can advise you on sleep training. Because you have already programmed your toddler to sleep at regular times, whichever method of sleep training you choose should work within seven to ten days.

Adjusting the routines

In my experience, the 7pm to 7am routine is the one that works best for the majority of babies and toddlers, though parents do manage to adjust the routines successfully so that they can get a lie-in at the weekend or have their toddlers up later in the evening. When adjusting the routines it is worthwhile bearing in mind that once your toddler or older child starts attending a regular playgroup or nursery school in the morning he will need to get up at 7am anyway if everything is to be fitted in. Allowing a child over 18 months to sleep later usually ends up with you having to dress him yourself because you are in a hurry. In the long run it is advisable to let him have the opportunity of learning this very important skill. Refer to page 9 for the importance of toddlers learning to dress themselves by 18 months. The following adjustments work with some toddlers but not all, so do not be disappointed if your toddler does not seem happy in a different routine.

The 7am – 7pm routine

A baby who has been following the original 7am – 7pm routine to the letter, will normally cut back on the early morning nap first. He will take longer and longer to drop off to sleep when he is put down for his nap at 9–9.30am. If your baby reaches a stage where he is only sleeping for 10–15 minutes at this time and getting through happily to his lunchtime nap, you could cut it out altogether.

The majority of toddlers will then continue to need a full two-hour sleep in the middle of the day until they are almost two years of age. Occasionally, some toddlers start to cut back on their lunchtime nap at around 18 months. They may sleep for two hours some days and only one-and-a-half hours on other days.

If your toddler does not sleep the full two hours but seems happy in his cot, I would advise you not to rush to him. A toddler who is used to quiet time alone will eventually learn how to relax and recharge without sleep. This can be a great help when he gets older and drops his nap altogether.

The 8am – 7pm routine

Many parents use this routine when their baby reaches one year. Others use the 7am – 7pm during the week and the 8am – 7pm routine at the weekend if they want a lie-in. Obviously, it will only work if your toddler still has to be woken at 7am or if he will settle himself back to sleep fairly quickly if he does wake at 7am. The darker the room, the more likely this is to happen. A toddler under 18 months who sleeps until 8am should not be allowed a morning nap, even if he normally has one on the 7am to 7pm routine. His lunch will need to be brought forward slightly so that he can go down for his two-hour nap not much later than 12.30 pm and be ready for bed at 7pm. A toddler of over 28 months who sleeps until 8am will probably manage to get through to 1 pm and then have a nap of no longer than one-and-a-half hours if you want him to be ready for bed at 7pm.

7am to 7.30/8pm

This routine is often used by working parents who want to spend a little extra time with their toddler on their return from work. It can work for many toddlers, but there is a greater risk of over-tiredness becoming a problem. To avoid this happening, the toddler should still be encouraged to have a nap in the morning, no matter how short. This will help him to get through to 1pm, when hopefully he will sleep for two hours. The short morning nap and the later lunchtime nap should help him manage to get through happily to the later bedtime of 7.30–8pm. If you find that your toddler is getting very tired on this routine, try alternating his bedtime so he is in bed slightly earlier every second night.

Routine for a toddler at 12–18 months

Mealtimes
Breakfast – 7/7.30am
Lunch – 12 noon
Tea – 5pm

Nap Times
Morning – 9.30–10am
Lunchtime – 12.30–2/2.30pm

Maximum daily sleep – two hours

7/7.30am
- Toddler normally wakes between 6.30 and 7am. He has a nappy change then a breast-feed or a cup of full fat milk from a beaker, followed by his breakfast solids.

8/8.30 am
- He should be happy to play by himself for a short time while you do a few things for yourself. I find this a good time to load the laundry and prepare part or all of his lunch.
- He should have his teeth cleaned and can be washed and dressed now if this did not happen earlier.

9/9.30am

- Depending on what time he woke up, he will now need a short nap of between 15 and 30 minutes. This often takes place in the car or the buggy on the way to the park or a playgroup. He should sleep no longer than 30 minutes if you want him to sleep well at lunchtime.
- He may need a small drink of water, well diluted juice and a small piece of fruit now if he had his milk and breakfast earlier. However, he should be offered this no later than 10am.

10am

- Toddlers' energy levels are at their peak at this time, and some sort of organised play will be needed if you wish to avoid boredom setting in. A trip to the park, local playgroup, swimming pool or some other social activity will work off some of his energy. If a trip out is not possible, he will certainly need some of your attention if he is to remain happily occupied in the house or garden.

11.30am

- Energy levels are beginning to dip now and hunger will be setting in. Try to allow enough time to get home and make or heat lunch up.

12 noon

- He can be given small pieces of fresh fruit or vegetables to chew on if he is showing signs of getting irritable while you are preparing or heating his lunch up. He should be given most of his solids before being offered a drink of water or well diluted juice.
- After his main course he should be encouraged to sit in the high chair and feed himself with a piece of fruit or cheese while you clear away the lunch things. If he is not interested in any more food, offer him a toy or book to play with while you clear up.
- Never leave your toddler unsupervised while he is in his high chair.

12.30pm

- He should be ready to go down for his big nap of the day around now. He will need to have his face and hands washed and nappy changed prior to going down.
- He will need a nap of no longer than two hours from the time he went down. If he slept until 7/7.30am and had a full 30 minutes in the morning, he may need slightly less sleep at this nap.

2.30/3pm

- He needs a breast-feed, a drink of milk, or some well diluted juice in a cup.
- Give him one small piece of fruit as a snack.

3pm

- If he had a very exhausting physical activity in the morning, try to arrange a quieter activity in the afternoon. If he had a quieter morning, try to encourage something more physical in the afternoon. A short walk in the park or a run around the garden to get some fresh air before teatime is always a good idea regardless of earlier activities, provided the weather allows.

5pm

- It is always a good idea to clear away most of the toys he has been playing with before he has his evening meal. A very active toddler can get a second wind after tea, and having too many toys out can make it difficult to get him upstairs for his bath. Also, some toddlers get very irritable and tired near bedtime, and tidying the toys away can become a battle.
- Always make sure that his hands are washed thoroughly before mealtimes, particularly after he has been playing outside. If your toddler has had his main protein meal at lunchtime, tea can be much simpler. Soup and sandwiches, pasta with a sauce and a selection of finger foods are good choices. He will need a drink of water, milk or well diluted juice with his tea, but try to encourage him to eat most of the solids before giving him the drink.

5.45/6pm

- Even if his bedtime is later than 7pm, it is a good idea to start the bedtime routine fairly soon after he has had his tea. He is at an age when he is capable of learning how to undress and dress himself (with help from you), so extra time should be allowed for this, as toddlers of this age tend to dawdle and get cross if rushed. He can also be encouraged to put his dirty clothes in the laundry basket and help lay out his clothes for the following day. As he nears 18 months he may also show signs of wanting to sit on his potty for a short spell. All of these things are part of his learning skills and help build his confidence and independence. Therefore it is very important to allow enough time so that you do not begin to get impatient with him.
- Toddlers usually take longer to bath than babies as they have developed more muscle control and hand–eye coordination, so water play features in the bath routine. They can also be given a small sponge or flannel and learn how to wash themselves.
- Allow between 10 and 15 minutes for drying, creaming and dressing. It is a good idea to encourage your toddler to participate actively in all of these things.
- Whenever possible, try to give your toddler his bedtime milk and story upstairs, as it can be very difficult to get him back upstairs if he has been taken down to the sitting room for this.

6.30/7pm

- Once your toddler is dressed and ready for bed it is important to dim the lights so that he realises it is now quiet time. Encourage him to choose the books and participate in the story telling. He can help turn the pages and point to and name the objects on the pages.
- Allow between 15 and 20 minutes for the bedtime drink and story telling – any longer than this can lead him to get a second wind and become difficult to settle. Before settling him to sleep always make sure that his teeth are thoroughly brushed and never allow him to finish his milk while falling asleep in the cot. This not only creates a bad sleep association but is a major cause of tooth decay.

- During this stage some toddlers get a bit clingy about being left. Playing a tape of gentle music or nursery rhymes will often help a toddler to settle.

Feeding
Once a baby reaches one year of age it is recommended that all drinks, including his milk, be given from a beaker. He now needs a minimum of 350ml (12oz) of milk a day and a maximum of 600ml (20oz). During the second year the rate at which your toddler grows will naturally slow down, and it is very common for toddlers suddenly to reduce the amount they eat. This is perfectly normal, but problems can occur if a toddler continues to have most or all of his meals puréed or is drinking excessive amounts of milk from a bottle. In my experience, it can be very difficult to get rid of the bottle after 15 months as toddlers seem to become even more dependent on it once they reach one year of age.

If you have not already done so, it is advisable to eliminate the bottle quickly and gradually introduce more finger foods if you have not already done so. Start to serve most of your toddler's food either mashed, chopped or sliced.

While it is very normal to see a decrease in appetite during the second year, food refusal can become a real problem if a toddler is allowed to continue drinking from a bottle or eating puréed food.

If you find that mealtimes are becoming a battle of wills, refer to pages 13–16 for advice on how to deal with this.

The day's menu for a toddler of between 12 and 18 months might look something like the following:

Breakfast
Breast-feed or 150/180ml (5–6oz) of full fat milk from a beaker

Breakfast cereal with milk and fruit or
Porridge with milk and fruit or
Baked beans on toast and/or
Toast fingers with butter or fruit spread and
Organic yoghurt and mashed or diced fruit

Mid-morning
Drink of water or well diluted juice from a beaker
Small piece of fruit

Lunch
Chicken and peach casserole with rice or mashed potato or
Fish in a creamy ribbon pasta sauce with carrots and sweetcorn or
Lamb hotpot with mini roast potatoes and peas or
Salmon and broccoli pasta with diced carrots or
Tuna risotto with mixed vegetables or
Fish cakes or fish fingers with potatoes and mixed vegetables

Yoghurt, fresh fruit, cheese and rice cakes
Drink of water or well diluted juice from a cup

Mid-afternoon
Drink of water or well diluted juice from a cup
Small piece of fruit or rice cake or plain biscuit

Tea
Baked potato with cottage cheese or
Vegetarian pizza and salad vegetables or
Thick minestrone soup and sandwiches or
Cauliflower/broccoli bake with mini roast potatoes or
Pasta and vegetables in a creamy sauce

Milk pudding, organic yoghurt and mashed fruit or
Piece of carrot or banana cake
120ml (4oz) of full-fat milk or water or well diluted juice from
   a cup

Bedtime
Breast-feed or 180ml (6oz) full-fat milk from a beaker

Sleeping
The majority of toddlers who are sleeping between 11 and 12
hours at night will still need two to two-and-half-hours of sleep
during the day, divided between two naps. However, by the time
your toddler reaches 18 months he should be able to get through
the day on one nap. Ideally, this nap should come after lunch, as

it will help him to get through the afternoon much better than a longer nap taken in the morning. Even if your toddler reaches 18 months and is sleeping well at night and at both his naps during the day, it is advisable to start to reduce and eliminate the morning nap gradually, particularly if he is going to start nursery school in the next few months. I have observed that toddlers who have been allowed to continue with two naps in the day past the 18-month stage often have great difficulty coping if they suddenly have to drop one when they start nursery school. If your child is one that appears to need more sleep, it would be better to allow him to sleep slightly later in the morning than to continue with two naps.

Development

Your toddler's coordination and manipulative skills improve rapidly during this stage and he will become increasingly more independent of you, wanting to feed himself, clean his own teeth and attempt to undress or dress himself. Although he will not always manage to do these things properly, his efforts should always be encouraged and extra time should be allowed at mealtimes and bedtimes to ensure that he has the chance to learn these things. He will go from cruising around the furniture at one year to walking steadily by 18 months. He will go from babbling and mimicking you to saying single words, and as his vocabulary increases he will start stringing two or three words together.

Listed below are some of the things that you can encourage your toddler to do at this stage:

- Drink all his milk and fluids from a beaker.
- Use a spoon to feed himself. Asking him which piece of food he is going to put on his spoon next, i.e. potato, carrot, cauliflower, etc. will help him learn the names of different foods.
- Dress and undress himself. Encourage him to put his dirty clothes in the laundry basket.
- Clean his teeth and wash himself. Asking him where his tummy or his knee is and then getting him to wash that particular part of his body will help him to learn the names of the different parts of his body.
- Walk upstairs holding your hand and come downstairs, either feet first on his tummy or step by step on his bottom.

Listed below are some of the toys and activities that will help your toddler develop:

- Chunky first stage crayons and big sticks of chalk.
- Shape sorters and simple jigsaws.
- Playdough.
- Books showing simple pictures of familiar things that encourage your toddler to look, point and name the object will help to develop his language skills and concentration. Lift the flap and touchy-feely books that your toddler can get involved with when you read to him are great for stimulating his imagination. By the time he reaches 18 months he will probably enjoy very simple short story books and nursery rhyme books with actions that he can join in with. When teaching your toddler a new word, always make sure that you speak slowly and clearly and that he is close enough to observe your mouth movements. Try not to teach him too many different new words at one time. Concentrate on a few words at a time and bring them constantly into everyday conversation with your toddler. Once he has mastered them select several more.
- Taking your toddler to a couple of activity classes a week will also help greatly with his developmental skills. He will learn a lot from playing alongside and watching the other children, eventually learning how to interact with other toddlers. A swimming class once a week is also a good way of improving his physical coordination and enabling him to expend lots of surplus energy.
- Hide and seek is great once your toddler is steady on his feet. It not only uses up lots of physical energy but also helps to develop your toddler's imagination and memory as he thinks of new places to hide.
- Push and pull along toys such as trikes, push along dogs, pull along animals, toy buggies, Hoovers, etc. help to develop your toddler's balance, coordination and manoeuvring skills, as well as teaching him to walk forwards while looking back, walk sideways and walk backwards confidently. They also help to develop his memory and imagination as he uses them in role-play, imitating the everyday activities that he observes going on around him.

- Action rhymes are great for helping to develop your toddler's physical coordination and at the same time improving his memory and language skills.
- Pretend play – with dolls, soft toys and pretend food, tea sets and household equipment – are great for helping toddlers understand the concept of sharing. How a toddler relates to his toys and interacts with others during pretend play can be an expression of how he is feeling emotionally. A toddler who learns to use his imagination through pretend or role-play will, as he gets older, find it easier to work out the solutions to problems. Activity toys or dolls with zips, buttons, poppers and fasteners are great for helping him learn to dress and undress himself.

Routine for a toddler at 18–24 months

Mealtimes
Breakfast – 7/7.30am
Lunch – 12/12.30pm
Tea – 5pm

Nap Time
12.30/1pm – 2/3pm

Maximum daily sleep – two hours

7/7.30am
- Toddler normally wakes between 6.30 and 7am, his nappy is changed and then he has a breast-feed or a cup of full-fat milk from a beaker, followed by his breakfast solids.
- Encourage your toddler to wash his own hands before and after eating (he will still need some help from you).

8/8.30am
- He should be happy to play by himself for a short time while you have some time to do things for yourself. I usually spend this time clearing up the breakfast things, loading the laundry and preparing part or all of his lunch.
- He should have his teeth cleaned and can be washed and dressed now if this did not happen earlier. He should manage

to put on most of his own clothes at this stage but will need help with buttons, etc.

9.30/10am
- Depending on what time he woke up and had his breakfast, he may now need a small drink of water or well diluted juice and a small piece of fruit.
- Try not to give drinks and snacks later than 10am, as this can take the edge off a toddler's appetite at lunchtime.

10am
- Toddlers' energy levels are at their peak at this time and some sort of organised play will be needed if you wish to avoid boredom setting in. A trip to the park, local playgroup, swimming pool or some other social activity will work off some of his energy. If a trip out is not possible, he will certainly need some of your attention if he is to remain happily occupied in the house or garden.
- Once or twice a week try to arrange to send him to a play-group or arrange a play date where he is left in the care of someone other than yourself. This will help to prepare him for starting nursery school.

12 noon/12.30pm
- Energy levels are beginning to dip now, and hunger will be setting in. Try to allow enough time to get home and organise or heat up lunch. If your toddler woke very early in the morning, you may have to bring his lunch forward by 10–15 minutes to avoid him becoming too tired to eat.
- He can be given small pieces of fresh fruit or vegetables to chew on if he is showing signs of getting irritable while you are heating his lunch up. He should be given most of his solids before being offered a drink of water or well diluted juice, and he should manage to eat most of his lunch by himself using a spoon. Try always to include some finger foods at lunchtime.
- After his main course he should be encouraged to feed himself with a piece of fruit or cheese while you clear away the lunch things. If he is not interested in any more food, offer him a toy or book to play with while you clear away the lunch things.

- He will probably be happiest sitting at a small table and chair specially designed for toddlers or in a booster seat attached to an adult chair. Never leave your toddler unsupervised while he is eating.
- Always remember to encourage him to wash and dry his own hands before and after the meal.

12.30/1pm
- He should be ready to go down for his big nap of the day around now. He will need to have his face and hands washed and nappy changed prior to going down.
- This nap should last no longer than two hours from the time he went down. If he slept until 7/7.30am or later in the morning, he may need slightly less sleep at this nap.

2.30/3pm
- He needs a breast-feed or a drink of milk or well diluted juice from a cup.
- Give him one small piece of fruit as a snack.

3pm
- If he had a very exhausting physical activity in the morning, try to arrange a quieter activity in the afternoon. If he had a quieter morning, try to encourage something more physical in the afternoon. A short walk in the park or a run around the garden to get some fresh air before teatime is always a good idea regardless of earlier activities, provided the weather allows.
- Encourage him to tidy away any toys that he has been playing with before he starts his tea.

5pm
- He should be given most of his solids before being offered a small drink of water or milk from a cup. It is still important that he has a good milk feed at bedtime, so keep this drink to a minimum.
- Try to ensure that he has some finger foods at this meal.
- Encourage him to say 'thank you' when he has finished his meal and help carry his empty bowl and beaker to the sink.
- Hands should always be washed before and after meals.

5.45pm

- Do not allow too much time between finishing tea and starting his bedtime routine. Toddlers of this age are very capable of getting a second wind and will be more tempted to start another round of activities if they remain downstairs among their toys.
- He can probably manage to walk upstairs one foot after the other, holding on to your hand.
- He should be able to take off nearly all of his clothes by himself at bath time and know by experience where the dirty linen basket is.
- He should be encouraged to sit on his potty for a short spell while the bath is being prepared.
- He will still need help with being dried and creamed, but once his nappy is on he should manage to put on his nightwear by himself, with some assistance with the buttons, etc.
- Give him two choices of outfit for the following day. Let him choose one and lay it out ready.

6.30/7pm

- Dim the lights so that your toddler knows this is quiet time. Encourage him to choose the books and participate with the story telling. He may now be able to follow a very simple storybook, with one or two lines to a page. He can help turn the pages and point to the objects and characters in the story.
- At this stage many toddlers try to drag bedtime out or change the bedtime ritual. It is important not to be sidetracked or give in to delaying tactics such as requests for just one more story or another drink of milk. Try to ensure that the bedtime drink and story last no longer than 15–20 minutes. If your toddler shows signs of being clingy, allow him to listen to a story or nursery rhyme tape for 20 minutes or so once he is in bed.
- He should be having all of his bedtime milk from a beaker, and his teeth should always be cleaned just before he goes to bed.
- It is also a good idea to get your toddler used to sitting next to you on the chair or bed while you are reading him his story. This helps prepare him for a different bedtime routine after the

arrival of a baby brother or sister, when it may not be possible to have him on your lap if you are trying to feed the baby at the same time as read to him.

Feeding

Your toddler still needs a minimum of 350ml (12oz) of full-fat milk a day in addition to solid food. This is usually divided between a drink in the morning and one at bedtime, with possibly a small drink at teatime. Many toddlers start to refuse their milk at this stage. If this happens, ensure that your toddler eats plenty of yoghurt, cheese and other foods high in calcium.

At this stage toddler eating habits can take a very erratic pattern. Some days they will eat masses and other days virtually nothing. Over a period of several days nearly all toddlers are getting the right balance of the different foods to meet their nutritional needs. If you are concerned as to whether your toddler is eating enough, try keeping a food diary. This will help you to decide whether his nutritional needs are being met. If you feel that they are not, it is advisable to discuss his eating habits with your health visitor.

The types of food you give your toddler will also affect his appetite greatly. Many yoghurts and cereals produced particularly for children are very high in sugars and additives, both of which can affect his appetite and cause him to refuse more healthy foods. Also limit how much juice and he has in between meals and the type of snacks. Try to allow a couple of hours between snacks and meals and choose fresh fruit or rice cakes as opposed to biscuits. Crisps, sausages, ham and other high-salt foods should still be avoided at this stage.

Your toddler should be feeding himself using a spoon at all of his meals now, although he will sometimes still be inclined to use his fingers as opposed to his spoon. Encourage him to use his spoon and praise him when he does, but try not to make too big a fuss when he doesn't. The most important thing is that he is keen to use it.

By the time he reaches two years of age he may be capable of using both a fork and a spoon to eat his meals, and he will be less likely to use his fingers. He can also on occasions be offered some of his drinks from a cup or beaker without a lid; however, be prepared for occasional accidents and try not to be too angry when these happen. If he is overtired or fractious, it is best to avoid using the cup and instead use a spouted beaker, as accidents are much more likely to happen when he is tired or upset.

He should be encouraged to participate in washing his own hands before a meal, and wiping his mouth and washing his hands after a meal. Install a small step beside the washbasin so that he can reach the taps himself. Supervise him so that he understands not to touch the hot tap.

Between 18 and 24 months his day's menu may look something like the following:

Breakfast
150–180ml (5–6oz) full-fat milk from a beaker
Breakfast cereal with milk and fruit or
Porridge with milk and fruit or
Baked beans on toast or
Scrambled egg on toast and/or
Toast fingers with butter or fruit spread
Organic yoghurt with mashed or diced fruit

Mid-morning
Drink of water or well diluted juice from a beaker
Small piece of fruit

Lunch
Baby Bolognese with green beans and sweetcorn or
Chicken and mushroom or apricot stir fry or
Mini salmon skewers or
Fishy ribbons and mixed vegetables or
Pork and apple casserole or
Salmon and broccoli quiche

Yoghurt, fresh fruit, cheese and rice cakes

Mid-afternoon
Drink of water or well diluted juice from a cup
Small piece of fruit or rice cake/plain biscuit

Tea
Kiddies' kedgeree or
Chinese noodles or
Mixed vegetable frittata or
Eggy bread with baked beans

Milk pudding or
Yoghurt and mashed or sliced fruit or
Carrot or banana cake
120ml (4oz) full-fat formula milk, water or well diluted juice
    from a beaker

Bedtime
Breast-feed or 180ml (6oz) full-fat formula milk

Sleeping
By 18 months the majority of toddlers are having only one
nap a day, having cut out the shorter morning nap and having
one long nap of usually one-and-a-half to two hours after
lunch.

If your toddler has been used to having his longer nap in the
morning and cuts out his shorter afternoon nap, he will get tired
much sooner than he used to at bedtime and probably fall into a
very deep sleep the minute he goes to bed. This may cause him to
start waking up earlier in the morning. In this case it would be
advisable gradually to cut down his morning nap by 10–15
minutes every few days so that he then needs a nap after lunch
again. Once he is sleeping only 10–15 minutes in the morning and
an hour or so after lunch, cut out the morning nap altogether, so
that his afternoon nap is hopefully between one-and-a-half and
two hours.

If your toddler cut out his morning nap before 18 months, he
may also cut down on his lunchtime nap sooner. Some days he
may sleep a full two hours, other days he may only need an hour,
depending on how active he has been. This sleeping pattern is
fairly normal as long as he is sleeping between 11 and 12 hours
at night. If he is cutting his night-time sleep back, which often
happens near the second birthday, you can try restricting his
daytime sleep to no more than one hour each day.

Development

During this stage your toddler will gain greater control of all his body movements. He will be able to walk confidently and steadily while holding on to a toy and walk backwards while pulling a toy along. He can now participate in games that involve stopping and starting, chasing and avoiding obstacles while running. He will be climbing up onto furniture to get to things out of reach and will be able to get himself back down again. He will also be capable of climbing up stairs and coming back downstairs two feet to a step, holding on to the handrail and jumping off the last step. He should manage to take off nearly all of his clothes and be capable of partly dressing himself, although he will still need help with button, belts, zips, etc.

Other physical skills he will learn at this stage are:

- Throwing and kicking a ball.
- Dancing to rhythmic music.
- Bouncing on a trampoline.
- Sitting astride a small trike or large toy on wheels and pushing himself forward with his feet.
- Opening door handles once he can reach them.
- Picking up small objects easily and turning pages of his books one at a time as his hand–eye coordination becomes more finely tuned. Scribbling will take the form of circles and dots now, not just random lines back and forth. He will also enjoy simple jigsaw puzzles that consist of three or four shapes, as well as peg-in bench toys and toy telephones, all of which will help develop his hand–eye coordination.

His vocabulary will increase rapidly at this stage, and he will be able to say 50 or more words and understand many more by the time he reaches his second birthday. He will start to string two or three words together to form short simple sentences. He will refer to himself by his name and can point to and often repeat the words for the different parts of his body. He will enjoy joining in with some of the words and actions of familiar songs and nursery rhymes.

It is important to be very descriptive when talking to your toddler as this will make verbal communication more enjoyable and teach him the art of conversation. Be aware, however, that talking often to your toddler will help to increase his vocabulary only if you also allow enough time for him to digest what you have been talking about.

When introducing new words include them in conversation as much as possible. When talking about familiar things and objects keep language as simple as possible and repeat the key words often. For example, if you are introducing the words 'big', 'small' and 'tiny', point out different objects and connect the word to the object. 'Look at that big car/small car/tiny car', etc. or 'big dog', 'small dog', 'tiny dog', 'big house', 'small house', 'tiny house'. Once he starts to understand the concept of the word you can then start to expand on the description, describing colour and other intricate details: 'the big black dog with the long tail'.

Your toddler will be able to follow short simple stories now, and including lots of story telling will also help to develop his communication skills. Choose books with two or three short sentences to a page and point out the key words in the story as you are reading to him. Involve him in the story telling by asking him to point out the different characters and colours and count the number of different objects on each page. For example: one dog, two cats, three trees, etc. Ask him which is bigger, the cat or the dog.

By the end of the second year your toddler will use his rapidly increasing imagination to imitate and copy people and situations that are part of his everyday life. He will use his toys to create his own imaginary world, of which he is in control. Role-play is a very important part of his development during a stage when his vocabulary is still limited. How he relates to his toys during role-play can portray how he sees the world around him. This form of play allows him to express many of the different emotions he is now beginning to experience but as yet does not fully understand.

Although your toddler will play independently in his own imaginary world, he will benefit greatly when you join in. By participating in the games he is creating you can help teach your toddler to understand more about his own feelings and those of others, and help him learn how to care and share.

Give him lots of praise when he is loving to his teddies and treats his toys with respect. For example, saying something like, 'Pooh bear loved that cup of tea, but what about poor Tigger? He looks very thirsty. Perhaps we can share some tea and biscuits with him as well.' When he offers Tigger the pretend cup of tea and biscuits, say how happy Tigger is to join in the tea party and what a clever boy he is for looking after all his friends.

Help to create rituals and routines in which all of his toys are treated thoughtfully and with kindness. For instance, each might have its own special place where it goes after play has finished. Dolly can sit in the bouncy chair, and Pooh and Tigger can share the pram. Encouraging him to treat his toys with respect in his imaginary world and not allowing him to throw them around or discard them carelessly at the end of play will encourage him to have respect for the people and things he comes into contact with in the real world.

Routine for a toddler at 24 to 30 months

Mealtimes
Breakfast – 7/7.30am
Lunch – 12/12.30pm
Tea – 5pm

Nap Time
1/1.30 pm – 2pm

Maximum daily sleep – one to one-and-a-half hours

7/7.30 am
- At this age a toddler normally wakes between 6.30 and 7.00am. If he is potty trained he should have his night-time nappy removed and be encouraged to sit on his potty for a few minutes before he is put into pants and taken down to breakfast. Many toddlers of this age will do a pee in their nappy when they first wake up so it is pointless leaving him on the potty for too long. If he is not potty trained, he should have his nappy changed.
- He should remember that his hands need to be washed after using the potty and before eating. If he keeps forgetting, add a column to his star chart to encourage him to take responsibility for this himself.
- He should have his breakfast no later than 7.30am, if his lunch is at 12.30pm. He can now alternate a drink of milk with

solids and he should be encouraged to place his cup down in between sips and while eating his breakfast.

- Encourage him to help clear away some of the breakfast things and to participate in wiping his mouth and washing his hands.
- Regardless of whether your toddler is potty trained or not, he should be sat on the potty for a short spell after breakfast. If he does not do anything, remind him where the potty is and that he should use it when he needs a pee or a poo.
- If he wasn't washed and dressed earlier, it is better to encourage him to do this now before he gets involved in playing with his toys. He should participate in teeth cleaning, washing and dressing, although he will still need some help from you.

8/8.30am

- He should be happy to play by himself for a short time while you do some things for yourself. I usually find this a good time to load the laundry and prepare part or all of his lunch. At this age toddlers often want to participate in household chores and this should not be discouraged, even if it means allowing longer to get tasks done.

9.30/10am

- Depending on what time he woke up, he will now need a small drink of water or well diluted juice and a small piece of fruit. Try not to offer snacks later than 10 am as this may put him off his lunch.
- Your child is probably attending a playgroup or is enrolled several mornings a week at a nursery. If he is having his snack there, it may be later than the time I recommend and you may notice a decrease in his appetite at lunchtime. If this is the case, you can try making his lunch at 1pm to see if this helps. If he is already having it at 1pm and is still not eating well, you can try giving him a lighter lunch of soup and a sandwich and then his bigger meal in the evening.

12.30/1pm

- He will either have a light lunch now or a full meal with protein, depending on his morning activities and how tired he is at midday. Whatever he has, he should be managing to eat it all without any help or prompting from you. He will probably be ready to use a fork and a spoon now as opposed to just a spoon, as well as drinking some of his drinks from a beaker or cup without a spout.

- He should be encouraged to put his cup down between sips and to rest his cutlery on the edge of the plate while he is eating.
- Encourage good manners at mealtimes by asking him to say, 'Thank you for the delicious meal' and 'Please may I leave the table?' Discussing the various foods and their names and why they are good for us while he is eating them will in time encourage him to appreciate the different tastes. This is the first stage to learning how to be appreciative of having a meal cooked for him.
- He should be encouraged to help not only with clearing up after lunch but also with laying out the things needed for lunch. Obviously, only ever allow him to carry unbreakable plates and beakers. He should not carry forks or knives at this stage in case he trips and hurts himself on one.
- If he is already potty trained, he should be encouraged to go on the potty before his lunchtime nap, but it is advisable to continue putting him in nappies for the nap.
- Hands should always be washed and teeth cleaned after the meal.
- He will need a nap now of between one and one-and-a-half hours. If he slept until 7/7.30am, he may need slightly less sleep at this nap. If he has cut right back on his daytime sleep it is advisable to encourage him to have quiet time in his room for at least an hour.
- If he has cut back on his night-time sleep and you are phasing his lunchtime nap out, he should still be encouraged to have some quiet time, preferably in his room.

3pm
- He needs a drink of water or well diluted juice from a cup.
- Give him a snack of one small piece of fruit.
- If he had a very exhausting physical activity in the morning, try to arrange a quieter activity in the afternoon. If he had a quieter morning, try to encourage something more physical in the afternoon. A short walk in the park or a run around the

garden to get some fresh air before teatime is always a good idea regardless of earlier activities, provided the weather allows.

- Before he starts his tea encourage him to tidy away any toys that he has been playing with.

5pm

- He should be given most of his breakfast before being offered a small drink of water or milk from a cup. The amount of fluid he drinks at this time can be increased provided he has eaten a good tea. When this happens he will probably reduce the amount he takes just prior to bedtime. This is an important step towards helping him to abandon night-time nappies once he is potty trained. A toddler who gets to three years of age and is still drinking 210–240ml (7–8oz) of milk at night is unlikely to manage to get through the night without needing to do a pee.
- Hands should be washed before and after meals.

5.45pm

- He should be taken upstairs no later than 5.45pm to avoid the possibility of him getting a second wind. Toddlers of this age become very assertive and can, if given the opportunity, become very difficult about going to bed.
- He should manage to walk up the stairs one foot after the other now and be confident about holding on to the banisters instead of your hand.
- He should manage to take all of his clothes off by himself but may still need help with zips and buttons, etc. He should not need reminding to put his dirty clothes in the linen basket, and he can even be encouraged to sort them out into different colours – whites, light colours, dark colours, etc. If he is reluctant to do this or keeps forgetting, it is another task that can be added to his star chart.
- Regardless of whether he is potty trained, he should be encouraged to sit on his potty while you are preparing the bath.
- He should be encouraged to help wash himself. Make a game of it and get him to name the different parts of his body as he is washing them.

- You will still need to help dry him, but he can participate in creaming parts of his body, and once his nappy has been put on he should manage to dress himself, getting help with buttons, etc.
- He should help to choose and lay out his clothes for the following day.

6.30/7pm

- Dim the lights so that your toddler knows that this is quiet time. Encourage him to choose a book and participate in the story telling. He will now be able to follow more complex stories, remembering the different characters and objects in the story and what happens on each page. He should manage to turn the pages one at a time.
- Even if he is managing to drink his milk from a beaker without a lid during the day, it is best to stick with a spouted one at bedtime for a while longer. If he is nearly three years of age, he should have gradually cut back on the amount he drinks at this time. If he is still drinking in excess of 240ml (8oz) I would advise that you gradually cut it back to nearer 220ml (7oz), otherwise it will be very difficult to get him out of night-time nappies when the time comes.
- Get him used to sitting next to you as opposed to sitting on your knee when reading the bedtime story. This will help to prepare him for a different bedtime routine if you are expecting a baby.
- If he has reached the stage where he is protesting about going to bed and using delaying tactics, it is important that you remain consistent. Do not allow him to lead you into a conversation that involves answering lots of questions. Keep repeating the same thing: that it is quiet time now and he must rest so that he is not too tired for – going to the park, play-school, swimming or whatever activity you have planned for the morning. At bedtime always try to leave him thinking about positive things that are going to happen the following day.

Feeding

Your toddler continues to need 350ml (12oz) of full-fat milk a day, although many toddlers do cut down dramatically the amount of milk that they drink at this age. If you find that your toddler is becoming very fussy about his milk or cutting it out altogether, you could try giving it to him in the form of milkshakes or smoothies. If this fails, offer your toddler plenty of yoghurt and cheese to ensure that his daily calcium requirements are being met.

He should manage to drink most of his drinks from a beaker without a spout at this stage, although it is advisable to continue with a spouted beaker for a while longer at bedtime.

At this stage the desire for sweets and chocolates can be a problem, particularly if your toddler is mixing with other children who are allowed them regularly. It is pointless to try to restrict them altogether, as this will only increase his desire for them. Allow them in moderation. While it is okay to use them as a reward, try never use them as a bribe.

It is possible to introduce bacon, sausages and other similar foods at this stage, but I would suggest that they are kept to a minimum.

Many toddlers who have always eaten their vegetables well, will start to get fussy about them. Try offering more salad vegetables or sticks of raw vegetables that can be served with a dip.

Your toddler should be self-feeding using his spoon and fork at this stage. Good table manners can be encouraged by teaching him to place his cup down between sips and his cutlery down on his plate while he is chewing. Remember, children learn best by example, so it is very important that you eat with your toddler on a regular basis.

Between 24 and 30 months his day's menu may look something like the following:

Breakfast
150ml (5oz) of full-fat milk from an open-top beaker or cup
Breakfast cereal with milk and fruit or
Porridge with milk and fruit or
Baked beans on toast or
Grilled chopped sausages with scrambled egg and/or
Toast fingers with butter or fruit spread and organic yoghurt
    with mashed or diced fruit

Mid-morning
Drink of water or well diluted juice from a beaker
Small piece of fruit

Lunch
Pork and apple casserole with mashed potatoes or
Salmon and vegetable stir fry or
Mini moussaka served with diced carrots and green beans or
Chicken and butter bean burgers served on a bread roll with
    lettuce, tomato and ketchup or
Fish Lyonnaise served with mixed vegetables or
Grilled lamb chops served with mashed potato or
Tuna and corn mayonnaise salad with potato wedges or
Beef and noodle stir-fry

Yoghurt, fresh fruit, cheese and rice cakes or
Drink of water or well diluted juice from a cup

Mid-afternoon
Drink of water or well diluted juice from a cup
Small piece of fruit of rice-cake/plain biscuit

Tea
Macaroni cheese with potato wedges or
Thick lentil and carrot soup served with mini sandwiches or
Pasta and vegetable gratin or
Savoury flan with shredded lettuce and salad vegetables or
Cheesy baked beans on toast or
Mushroom omelette or
Vegetable and noodle stir-fry

150ml (5oz) full-fat milk or well diluted juice or water from
    a beaker
Milk pudding, carrot, orange or banana cake or
Yoghurt and fresh fruit

Bedtime
150–180ml (5–6oz) full-fat milk from a beaker

Sleeping

By two years of age the majority of toddlers are having one nap a day of between one and two hours. By the time they reach two-and-a-half years of age their daily sleep requirements usually drop to 12–13 hours a day, and some children who need less sleep will cut right back on their lunchtime nap, sometimes only needing a nap every second or third day.

If your toddler cuts back on the lunchtime nap, he will probably need to be in bed no later than 7pm to avoid becoming overtired. It is around this age that many toddlers also attempt to climb out of their cot. I would suggest that you watch your child very closely. If you think he might be able to succeed in climbing out, it would be safer to transfer him to a bed. Once he is in a bed it is important to ensure that his room is totally childproofed, and if he persists in getting out of the bed and is able to get out of his room, you may have to fit a stair-gate across the doorway. Invest in a very strong one that can be fixed a few centimetres up from the ground so that it is high enough to prevent him from climbing over.

Many toddlers of this age start to have fears about sleeping in the dark. This is perfectly normal, and when it happens it is advisable to leave on a very low plug-in socket light, as no child of this age should be forced to sleep in the dark.

Development

By two-and-a-half years of age your toddler's energy will seem endless. He will be running, climbing and jumping with great skill and ease. His sense of balance will also be improving, and he will be more confident about using climbing frames unassisted. He will be much more capable of throwing and catching a ball and he will also be beginning to understand the rules of simple ball games. His finer body movements and eye–hand coordination will also be greatly improved so that drawings and paintings begin to take some form and shape. He is fascinated by switches, knobs, telephones, etc., and quickly learns how to use these. He can usually unfasten his seatbelt, buggy straps and so on, so extra care must be taken. His concentration is also improving and he will spend longer on creative activities before getting bored.

He will be talking non-stop at this age, particularly during imaginary play with his toys. He will probably have a vocabulary of nearly 200 words at 30 months, and his conversation will take on a more adult tone, although he will still revert to baby language when upset or tired. Stuttering is not uncommon at this age, and is, again, more likely to happen when he is upset or tired.

He can also remember simple things now, being able to relate to a story you read to him a few nights ago and join in with most of the words and actions of short nursery rhymes and songs. He will also begin to have a better understanding of numbers and be able to recognise different colours.

Routine for a toddler at 30–36 months

Mealtimes
Breakfast 7/7.30am
Lunch 12.30/1pm
Tea 5pm

Nap Time
1/1.30pm – 2/3pm

Maximum daily sleep – 45 minutes

7am
- Your toddler will normally wake between 6.30 and 7am. When he wakes he should have his night-time nappy removed and be encouraged to sit on the potty or the loo for a few minutes before he is put into his pants and taken downstairs.
- He should now be in a routine where he knows he needs to wash his hands after he has done a pee and always before he eats his meals. Use a star chart to reinforce these habits if he is constantly having to be reminded.
- He should have breakfast no later than 7.30pm if his lunch is at 12.30pm. He should manage to drink his breakfast milk from a cup without a lid and will want to alternate between drinking and eating at breakfast. He should now be getting used to setting his cup down between sips and his cutlery down while he is chewing his food.
- He should help to clear away the breakfast things and remember that his mouth needs to be wiped and his hands washed after the meal.

- He may need to use his potty or the loo fairly soon after breakfast, and if he has just recently been potty trained he may need a gentle reminder to do this.
- If he was not washed and dressed earlier, this should be done now, before he gets engrossed in other activities. He will still need help with washing and teeth cleaning, but he should manage to put on all his clothes by himself, with help with difficult buttons.

8/8.30am

- He should be happy to play by himself for a short time while you do some things for yourself. I usually find this a good time to sort out domestic chores and prepare his lunch. He may often want to assist you with these, and this should not be discouraged, even if it means taking longer to get tasks done.

9/9.30am

- Depending on what time he woke up, he will now need a small drink of water or well diluted juice and a small piece of fruit. Try not to offer snacks later than 10am as it may put him off his lunch.
- At this stage your toddler is probably attending a playgroup or is enrolled several mornings a week at nursery. If he is having his snack there, it may be later than the time I recommend and you may notice a decrease in his appetite at lunchtime. If this is the case, you can try making his lunch at 1pm to see if this helps. If he is already having it at 1pm and is still not eating well, you can try giving him a lighter lunch of soup and sandwiches and then his bigger meal in the evening.
- Toddlers' energy levels are at their peak at this time and some sort of organised play will be needed if you wish to avoid boredom setting in. A trip to the park, a local playgroup, the swimming pool or some other social activity will work off some of his energy. If a trip out is not possible, he will certainly need some of your attention if he to remain happily occupied in the house or garden.

11.30am

- Energy levels are beginning to dip now and hunger will be setting in. Try to allow enough time to get home and heat lunch up.

12.30/1pm

- He will either have a light lunch now or a full meal with protein, depending on his morning activities and how tired he is at midday. Whatever he has, he certainly should be managing to eat it all without any help or prompting from you. He will probably have progressed from using a spoon and fork to a specially designed chunky knife and fork suitable for toddlers and young children.
- Although he will probably still need to wear a large apron while eating, it is a good idea to introduce a napkin and teach him how to wipe his own mouth during the meal.
- He should now have an understanding of basic table manners but will continue to need gentle encouragement and reminders for quite a while yet. Putting his cup down between sips, laying his cutlery down while chewing his food and not talking while he has food in his mouth are all things that he should be made aware of at this age.
- Always encourage him to discuss the meal and teach him the importance of thanking whoever cooked it.
- Helping clear up after lunch should now be a habit, and helping to set the table for lunch should also be encouraged.
- Hand washing before and after lunch should be well established.

12.30/1pm

- The majority of toddlers will have cut right back or dropped their lunchtime nap by now, but quiet time should still be encouraged after lunch, particularly if your toddler is at nursery school every morning.

3pm

- He needs a drink of water or well diluted juice from a cup.
- Give him a snack of one small piece of fruit.
- If he had a very exhausting physical activity in the morning, try to arrange a quieter activity in the afternoon. If he had a quieter morning, try to encourage something more physical in the afternoon. A short walk in the park or a run around the garden to get some fresh air before teatime is always a good idea regardless of earlier activities provided the weather allows.

4.30pm

Children can often become demanding at this time of day when both mother and child are becoming tired. To avoid any difficulties, I would encourage half an hour of creative play while you prepare tea. If your toddler is doing an activity at the kitchen table, you can prepare the meal without distraction. Do try to avoid answering the phone at this time of the day, when your child's behaviour is most unpredictable.

Most children love a little colouring, stickering or playdough. Once you have discovered what your child prefers, this is a great time to encourage them.

Give him his tea promptly, ideally no later than 5pm. If possible, sit with him while he eats, so that you can encourage good table manners and help where appropriate. Children eating on their own while their mother tidies up the kitchen are more likely to play with their food, make a terrible mess and prolong mealtime.

Normally children have a burst of energy after they have eaten, and this is good time to encourage them to help you tidy up toys or sweep the floor. It is a good idea to direct the child's behaviour through play.

At this time your toddler will be tired, and accidents as well as naughty behaviour are more likely, so it is important to be extremely patient if bedtime battles are to be avoided.

5.45pm

Aim to be upstairs no later than 5.45pm, as the bed- and bath time routine will be much more fun and relaxing if you allow plenty of time.

Most children love their bath, and this is all part of the bedtime ritual, but remember to choose bath toys that are fun and educational but will not cause your child to become over-excited.

6/6.15pm

While you will still have to dry your child, he can continue to help with creaming and should be encouraged to put on his own nightclothes. Pyjamas are best at this age, as you can leave putting on the night-time nappy until just prior to putting him to bed.

Help your toddler to choose the bedtime stories that he wants to hear and encourage him to join in with naming the characters and finishing the sentences in stories he is familiar with. Try always to read stories with a positive note and avoid any that may cause nightmares. Set a strict time for how long you read to him and avoid getting into the habit of just one more story.

Once he has finished his milk he should clean his teeth (with your help) then sit on his potty one last time before his night-time nappy is put on. It is worth paying a little extra for a top-of-the-range night-time nappy that absorbs more urine so that your child's bottom remains dry and free from soreness. Applying a little bit of Sudocream to the creases is also a good idea if your child has sensitive skin.

7/7.30pm

Settle your child in his bed with no more than one or two of his favourite toys. Kiss them all good night and be very firm about not getting into the habit of going back time and time again to say goodnight.

If your child says he is not ready to sleep, tell him that it's okay for him to stay awake a bit longer, but he must lie and rest, as it is quiet time now.

You can leave the night-light or his bedside light on if he wants to read a story by himself or listen to a music tape.

Feeding

Between 30 and 36 months your toddler will be eating almost everything that is enjoyed by the rest of the family. Your toddler's daily menu may look something like the following:

Breakfast
150ml (5oz) full-fat milk from an open-top beaker or cup
Breakfast cereal with milk and fruit or
Muesli with milk and chopped fruit or
Porridge with milk and fruit or
Baked beans and scrambled egg on toast or
Grilled diced bacon or chopped sausage with tomato and poached
   egg or
Grilled kipper, deboned and chopped with scrambled egg or
Toast fingers with butter and fruit spread or

Pancakes with fruit and yoghurt mix or
Organic yoghurt with mashed and diced fruit

Mid-morning
Drink of water or well diluted juice from a beaker
Small piece of fruit or dried fruit, or savoury biscuit

Lunch
Chicken and apricot stir-fry or
Salmon and pasta salad with baby new potatoes or
Grilled lamb chops served with mini roast potatoes and
    cauliflower cheese or
Chicken paella or
Cod and corn fishcakes served with diced potatoes and mixed
    vegetables or
Beef meatballs in tomato and herb sauce with fresh vegetables
    and wedge potatoes or
Tuna and egg salad with homemade chips

Yoghurt, fresh fruit, cheese and rice cakes
Drink of water or well diluted juice from a cup

Mid-afternoon
Drink of water or well diluted juice from a cup
Small piece of fruit or rice cake/plain biscuit

Tea
Thick minestrone soup with mini sandwiches or
Pizza slices with sticks of raw vegetables or
Creamed vegetable risotto or
Vegetable omelette with wedge potatoes or
Pasta and vegetables in tomato sauce or
Baked potato with a choice of fillings

Drink of full-fat milk or well diluted juice or water from a beaker
Milk pudding, muffins, fruit scones, or fruit crumble and cream or
Cheese and biscuits or
Fresh fruit and yoghurt

Bedtime
150–180 ml (5–6oz) of full-fat milk from a beaker

Sleeping

By three years of age the majority of children will have cut out their daytime nap altogether. Children of this age are using an awful lot of energy both mentally and physically; therefore it is important that they get enough sleep at night. If your toddler is used to a later bedtime of nearer 8pm, you may find that you have to bring it forward slightly once he drops his daytime nap.

A move from the cot to a bed will also take place during this stage if it has not already taken place, and the bedtime routine can sometimes fly right out the window if you are not consistent and persistent when settling your child. At this age many young children will keep trying to change the bedtime rituals and the settling time begins to take longer and longer. Be very firm about how long you read to your toddler at bedtime. When it comes to saying goodnight, do not get talked into just one more story or just one drink. If necessary, allow your child to have his bedside light on for a short period after you say goodnight. He can read a story or listen to a music tape, but he should be allowed this only if he is prepared to settle quietly in his room. He is at an age now where he must be given choices and learn that there are consequences to his choices. For example, he is not expected to go straight to sleep and he can have the light on and read a story by himself, but only if he does so quietly and does not get out of bed and make a lot of noise. If he chooses to get out of bed and make a noise, then he must accept the consequence that the door will be shut and the light turned off. By having the choice he will feel in control and quickly realise which is the better option. Of course, he will only realise the consequences of his actions if you follow through with actually shutting the door and turning off the light should he decide to be noisy and refuse to settle by himself.

Once the daytime nap is dropped I would suggest that you still encourage quiet time after lunch. Some children will happily go to their room for an hour or so and play quietly or read a book. If your child is not keen to do this, you should still insist that everything be kept low-key and quiet should he want to stay downstairs. Some young children will lie down for a rest on the sofa for half an hour or so. If your child refuses to do this, he should be encouraged to entertain himself for the quiet period. It is important that he realises you are not there to entertain him every waking hour and that you also need a rest. This is particularly important if you have just had a second baby. By ensuring that you get this rest time every day you will have much more energy to do something with him later in the afternoon. This is impossible if you have been on the go non-stop since breakfast time.

Development

Your toddler's physical coordination will continue to improve and he will now become much more confident about joining in physical games with children his own age. His hand–eye co-ordination will also have improved and he will be much more able to feed himself using cutlery and drink from an open-top cup without accidents happening.

Encourage lots of creative play to enhance these skills. He should manage to do drawing and colouring in with much more precision. Buy him more complicated jigsaws and puzzles at this stage and encourage him to cut out shapes using child-friendly scissors and form his own pictures of places that you have visited together.

This is a great age to start an A to Z food diary, in which he draws the different types of food and understands their shapes and colours. Each week plan a simple recipe for the different foods, write it up in his diary and get him to help you shop for the ingredients and cook the meal. Making the meal a special occasion when other friends or relations come to join in will encourage your child to take an interest in food and try different things.

It is important that you resist doing things for your child because you are in a hurry. Try to allow longer for getting dressed, hand washing, etc. Your child is at an age now where he is capable doing these things for himself. It is important to allow him the opportunity to take responsibility for himself. He should also have regular little tasks to do and be given lots of encourage-ment and praise when doing them.

During this stage you can encourage caring behaviour by creating a tiny patch in the garden where he can be taught to grow and care for a few plants. Buying him a small pet such as a goldfish and encouraging him to take responsibility for it is another way of teaching him how to care for others.

If you have not already implemented a star chart, now is a good time to do so. Encouragement, praise and rewards will help your child develop into a kind, considerate and tolerant human being much more than criticism, threats and punishment. Remember always to accentuate the positive and eliminate the negative.

6

The New Baby

A question I am frequently asked by parents considering trying for a second child is, 'What is the ideal age gap between children?' Having worked with so many different families, I have come to the conclusion that the age gap between the children is not as important as ensuring that the couple themselves are both in agreement that they can cope physically, emotionally and financially with a second baby.

When deciding whether the time is right to start trying for a second baby, you and your partner should discuss fully and honestly the following issues. It is important that you are both in agreement about these and express honestly any worries that you may have about coping with an addition to the family.

Physical and emotional issues

It is important that you discuss how you will cope with caring for two children on a day-to-day basis. Caring for a toddler and a new-born baby can be both physically and emotionally exhausting, particularly if you do not have an extended family close at hand to help out and give support. I hear from many young mothers who feel exhausted and isolated when a second baby arrives. This often happens because they have had to relocate to a new area because of their partner's job or a recent promotion means their partner has to work later in the evening. Arguments and resentment occur because the mother feels she is totally alone caring for two young children day and night. The husband often becomes stressed from having to work longer and carry what may be the new financial responsibility of being the sole provider for family. What precious spare time both partners have in the evening is often spent arguing about who is the most exhausted. Observing and discussing with friends how they cope with a second baby can be a great help. Offering to baby-sit their children for a few hours at weekends will also give you an idea of what is involved in caring for more than one child. If you have helped out with their children, they will also be more likely to offer you help when you have your second baby.

It would be wise for you both to have a medical check-up with your GP and a chat to ensure that you are both physically fit. This is particularly important for a mother who had a difficult birth or a caesarean the first time.

I appreciate that for women who had their first child later in life choosing the right time to have a second is not an option, as time is running out. If you think that you will be in a situation where your partner will not be able to give you the amount of physical help you would ideally like, it would be wise to ensure that you get help and support from elsewhere. It is very important not to become physically exhausted, which in turn will leave you mentally drained and put a strain on yourself and the whole family.

Financial issues

Shortage of money is one of the main things that couples argue about. If you have to move house to accommodate a second child, it is important to work out your finances carefully so that you know that the extra outgoings each month are not going to put too much pressure on you. You will also need to include the expense of any renovations, decoration and repairs that will arise with a house move, and the cost of furnishing another bedroom for the new baby.

If your first child is over the age of three years you will not have the major expense of buying the basic baby equipment. However, if you are planning to have a closer age gap, there will be the expense of a double buggy and perhaps a second cot, and you will probably find that you will be buying nappies for two for many months to come. Although these may seem just small points, they will increase your expenses by a sizeable amount.

Returning to work after your first child is often a possibility, but a second child makes matters more complicated and it can be difficult for the mother to return for a second time. Having to cope with one income instead of two along with the added expense of a second baby may mean that for a couple of years money for luxuries, such as holidays and meals out, is not so readily available. It is important that you are both happy about making these sacrifices, otherwise resentment of the change in lifestyle could become a big problem.

If you both plan to continue to work – even if one of you is only working part-time – it is important to calculate the amount needed for childcare, not just the amount paid to the carer but also the extra needed for travel and trips out, and all the expenses the carer will expect you to pay for. If you are considering employing a nanny, you will also be responsible for her insurance and tax and for providing her meals when she is on duty.

I have seen many young couples go through absolute misery the first year or so after a second baby. All the joy is taken away from family life simply because they did not do their sums correctly.

Age gap – what to expect

Whether or not you achieve the age gap you are aiming for (and you may not have had a choice in the matter) there will always be some difficulties in the early days after a new baby arrives. With a little foresight and forward planning these difficulties can be kept to the minimum and overcome fairly quickly. In my experience, parents who have worked out a plan in advance for how they are going to deal with these different hurdles are likely to have fewer disputes and cope better with the extra addition to the family.

Close together (a 10–15-month age gap)

Having an age gap of 10–15 months is very similar to having twins in terms of feeding and sleeping and general day care. Both children will still be in nappies, and the toddler will still need some assistance with feeding and still need to be lifted and carried some of the time. The day can often seem like an endless succession of feeding, changing and getting nap times right. It is often much harder to get out and about with two such young children, as the logistics of a double buggy and loading it up with all the gear can be fairly daunting.

The upside of having such a close age gap is that children under 15 months do not appear to be so jealous of the new baby, and as they get older there appears to be less sibling rivalry when they are playing together.

If you are planning to have only two children another advantage is that you get out of the baby mode of nappy changing, buggy pushing and preparation of baby food much quicker. Within three years you can be back to enjoying a wider range of social activities and holidays, as you will not be so restricted by sleep requirements and the need to lug so much equipment on outings and holidays.

Average age gap (18 months to three years)

Eighteen months to three years appears to be the most popular age gap. There is often a certain amount of jealousy when the new baby arrives, but keeping the toddler's routine consistent and ensuring that he gets special time every day usually prevents things getting out of hand.

In my experience, it is always more difficult when the toddler is aged between 18 months and two years, probably because this is a period when he is learning so many different new skills. Talking, potty training and getting dressed are major hurdles in a toddler's life. He needs a lot of encouragement and help in learning these skills, and can become very frustrated trying to learn so many different things. A mother coping with a new baby can often find it difficult to remain patient when teaching these things, and the toddler quickly picks up on his mother's tension. A mixture of the toddler's frustration and the mother's tension creates a ripe ground for toddler tantrums. With this age gap getting the baby into a good routine is paramount, as it will mean that you have the time needed to help your toddler cope with learning the different skills.

It is very important that the toddler realises you love him just as much as before the baby came along and that during each day there are still little slots where it is just you and him. Ensuring that he has learnt as many of the skills possible for his age and encouraging a certain amount of independence before the baby arrives will also help things go more smoothly.

When the toddler is nearer to two-and-a-half, things are less fraught than they are at 18 months or so. By this time they have learnt more skills and having a toddler and a baby is less tiring for the mother. A toddler's communication skills are better by now and he is able to understand when you tell him you love him just as much as before the arrival of the baby.

Big age gap (three or more years)

When there is an age gap of three years or more the biggest hurdle is in the parents and elder child having to revert back to a more restricted social life. Getting back into baby mode, particularly arranging things around the baby's sleep times, can take some adjusting to for everyone. The older the first child is when the baby is born, the more difficult it is to arrange family outings that are of interest to both the baby and the child.

However, the upside is that there is usually little or no jealousy, as the older child is usually fairly independent and will have established a circle of friends, so the baby is not a threat to his daily routine. This may not be the case if the elder child is used to spending much of his social times with his parents instead of children his own age. If there is going to be a big age gap, it is very important to ensure that your elder child has a wide circle of friends his own age, otherwise jealousy could become a real issue. It will also be easier for parents to divide their time between a much older child and a young baby. The mother is able to devote lots of time to the baby during the day when the elder child is at nursery or school, and a later bedtime for an elder child ensures that parents can devote their undivided time to him in the evenings, provided the baby is in a good routine and settles well in the evening.

Help with your new baby

If you anticipate little or no help from your extended family after the baby is born, it is advisable to look at other ways to help you cope with two children. Many mothers feel guilty about seeking help, believing that they should be able to cope on their own and that having help with children is a luxury for the rich. But this is not the case. In the past the majority of young mothers got help from grannies and aunties as a matter of course. With more and more families living further and further apart from each other, and more grannies working full-time themselves, it has become harder for today's young parents to cope in the early months after a baby has been born, even more so when a second or third child comes along. I believe that getting help in the early days should be seen as a necessity for all parents, not a luxury.

Getting help for three or four hours a week can make a huge difference, even if it is only on a short-term basis. If your budget will allow getting someone in to clean the house once a week or watch the children while you have some 'you' time which will allow you to step back from the situation.

It is very easy to become overwhelmed when looking after two young children and trying to create a happy family life, and ensuring that everyone's needs are being met often means that mothers always put themselves last. Being a good mother should not mean becoming a martyr.

If you are on a tight budget, the following are options for getting help after the new baby arrives:

- Local colleges that run courses for training nursery nurses and nannies and are always looking for families where they can place young girls one day a week as part of their practical training. While these young girls have to be carefully supervised, they can be a marvellous help, playing with the elder child or taking both children to the park for a walk. They can also help out at mealtimes and bath times, which are always hectic when the second baby arrives.
- Setting up a baby-sitting circle with other young mothers is another way of getting some 'you' time. It usually works better with at least three mothers, so that there are always two mothers looking after all of the children while the third mother has her time out. It is always a great way of helping both your elder child and your baby become outgoing, sociable little people.
- Sure Start is a governmental organisation that provides help a few hours a week to young mothers. Volunteers come and help out with children or will do the weekly shop, etc. This charity helps mothers from all sorts of backgrounds, not just parents on very low incomes. They are well known for helping young

families who have relocated and have not yet built up a network of friends in their new area.

Routine and rituals

Before the new baby arrives you should look closely at your toddler's routine, especially any rituals that take place in the morning and at bedtime. If you have to alter any of them, try to make it not seem as if the arrival of the baby is the cause of the changes in his life. For example, if he is used to sitting on your knee for his bedtime story, try to get him used to sitting next to you instead. This will make it possible for you to feed the baby at the same time as you are reading him his story. Mealtimes may need to be altered slightly to fit in with breast-feeding, as will the time of the bath.

Listed below are further suggestions for how to prepare your toddler for the arrival of a new baby:

- The more skills your toddler has learned before the baby arrives, the easier it will be for you to cope with the demands of two children. The majority of toddlers are capable of self-feeding by 18 months and undressing themselves by 30 months. A toddler who is still dependent on you to help him with these things will get very resentful if you expect him suddenly to start doing them for himself after the baby is born.

- Try to get your toddler used to entertaining himself for short spells while you do necessary chores. Introduce play activities such as jigsaws, drawing, finger painting and playdough. Both boys and girls will benefit from having their own special baby doll, complete with feeding bottle, nappies, bath and Moses basket.

- Avoid major changes in your toddler's life prior to the birth or after the baby is born. It can take several weeks for a toddler to settle in to nursery, so try to organise his starting date either several weeks before the birth or several weeks after the baby has arrived. If you need his cot for the new baby, try to put him in his new bed at least two months before the baby arrives.

- Try to arrange that your partner and toddler get used to

having short spells alone together at the weekend. This way your toddler will not feel you are suddenly abandoning him when you have much needed rest during the early weeks of breast-feeding.

- Get your toddler used to babies by inviting friends with babies to visit. Discuss how small and fragile they are, also how noisy they can be when they cry. Read books that explain about babies being born and having a new baby in the family.

Adapting your routine to fit in with a new baby

The arrival of a new baby does present new demands and challenges, and it is only natural to feel concerned that it will be difficult to cope with two children and their different daily needs. If you have already used the routines in *The New Contented Little Baby Book* successfully with your first child, then it may seem that the task ahead will be impossible. However, a new baby can easily adapt to suit his sibling's routine, and the difficulties that sometimes hinder a first baby falling into my routine rarely present themselves with the second child.

In those early days with a new baby, one of the most challenging aspects of the *Contented Little Baby* routines is ensuring that the baby has its first feed at 7am. If the baby wakes during the night and is sound asleep at 7am, it is natural for a new mother to want to lie in and wake when the baby wakes. This may even mean that the baby doesn't have its first feed of the day until after 9am. The knock-on effect is that it is impossible for the mother to ensure that the baby has the right amount of milk during the day, and as a result, the baby will wake at night to top up. However, those mothers who already have a toddler are rarely given a lie-in, and beginning the day at 7am is completely natural. Within a very few days the baby has become accustomed to the 7am feed, and the pattern for achieving a contented little baby is already in place.

A toddler who is following the routines in this book is the ideal companion for a new baby. An older brother or sister provides the most perfect distraction to a new baby during its wakeful times. The most sophisticated play-gyms are no match for the exuberant noises, silly faces and happy antics of a contented two-year-old. Similarly, the rest times encouraged for a toddler coincide with the daytime sleep of a new baby. The meal-times can be organised so that the baby is fed consecutively, and the bath time routine is already in place. Trips to the park, walks to nursery and visits from friends can all be planned to coincide with the routines. Of course, a little flexibility is needed in minor aspects. If a mother needs to collect her toddler from nursery at 12 noon, it is impossible for her to be settling the baby in the cot at this time. However, with a little tweaking the routine falls into place: the new baby has a prompt feed and, if on solids, these are fed before 11.30am. This enables the mother to collect her two-year-old after the baby has been fed. The baby will be ready to fall asleep en route to nursery, and if this happens he can be safely transferred to his cot on the return home. If you find you have problems settling your baby back in his cot, I would suggest that you give him a quick top-up of 60–90ml (2–3oz) of milk, which should ensure that he goes back to sleep without too much difficulty.

Example of a routine for a toddler and three-month-old baby

7am
- The baby will need to be fed and then encouraged to sit in his chair while the toddler has his breakfast.
- If your baby wakes before 7am, give him a feed from one breast and settle him back to sleep. It would then be best to wake him and give him the second breast while the toddler is having his breakfast.
- Try to get both children fed by 8am, so that you allow plenty of time for washing and dressing.

8–10 am
- Get both children washed and dressed.
- The baby will be ready for a nap between 8.30 and 9am or two hours after he last woke. If you have to take the toddler to nursery, this nap will have to take place in the car or the buggy.
- Once you have dropped the toddler off at nursery, time

permitting you can probably fit in a little shopping or a walk. This will ensure that the baby sleeps well during his morning nap.

10am–12.30pm
- The baby will need a feed somewhere between 10 and 11am, and will probably be ready for a nap between 11.30am and 12 noon.
- Once he has had his feed, encourage him to go on her play-mat for a short spell so that you can fit in a few chores and prepare lunch for you and your toddler.

11.30am/12noon
- The baby will be ready for a nap around now. If you have to pick your toddler up from nursery, he will have to take the first part of his nap in his car seat or buggy. But try to prepare his cot room so that he can go straight down in his cot the minute you get home.

12.30–2pm
- Having settled your baby into his cot you can then have lunch with your toddler. If you have problems settling the baby back in his cot at this time, a quick top-up of 60ml (2oz) milk should do the trick. During this stage of development your toddler will benefit greatly if you try to make time to eat with him. It will also help him realise that although he now has to share you with his baby brother or sister, he still gets special time with mummy.
- Even if your toddler has dropped his midday nap, try to encourage him to have some quiet time after lunch. Noisy games and running around should be discouraged. This will allow time for both you and him to recharge your batteries and ensure that the baby has a really good sleep at lunchtime.

2pm–6pm
- Aim to have the baby awake and feeding no later than 2pm, so that he has had at least half of his feed during your toddler's nap or quiet time. By 2.30pm your toddler will probably be starting to get a bit restless, so it will become very difficult if he has to sit through nearly an hour of you feeding the baby.

- Once he is up he will probably be happy to play with some of his toys while you finish off the baby's feed. If he is demanding your attention, try reading him a story while you finish off the feed.
- This is also a good time to offer him a drink and a snack.
- He will most certainly be getting bored by 3pm so try to arrange different things to do each afternoon in advance – a trip to the park, an arranged activity or a play date with some of his friends. Alternate the activities so that he does not have really hectic ones two or three days in a row. If he is at nursery school every morning, afternoon activities should be more relaxed ones, so that overtiredness does not become a problem at bedtime.
- The baby will need a short nap between 4 and 5pm. This can be taken in his buggy during a trip to the park, or if at home in the garden or a quiet room downstairs.
- If the play date is taking place at home, I would advise that you get the other mothers to help you put the bulk of the toys away at 4.30pm. The fewer toys there are to clear up, the easier it will be to get the toddlers to cooperate at clearing them away, at a time when they are beginning to get tired and hungry.
- The baby will need to have a half of his breast-feed or bottle around 5pm. Depending on what you have been doing that afternoon, you should aim to give your toddler his tea at either 5 or 5.30pm. If he has friends around, he may be happy to play on until 5.30pm, allowing you to feed the baby. The baby, having been fed, will be happy to sit in his bouncy chair or go on the play-mat while you prepare and give tea to the toddler. Alternatively, if you have been very organised and prepared tea earlier, some toddlers will be happy to sit and eat their tea while the baby is being fed.
- It is important that if you are feeding the baby at the same time that your toddler is having his tea, you do so in a seat very close to your toddler. A small toddler should never be left alone while eating. Not only is it dangerous but it will also lead him to feel very abandoned if you go off to another room to feed the baby.

6–7.30pm

- This is usually one of the most difficult times of the day for parents with a young baby and a toddler. The majority of young babies and toddlers are getting tired and irritable by this time. Trying to get them both bathed and settled happily in their beds at a reasonable time requires a huge amount of patience and discipline from the parents. Through my experience with working with mothers and their families I have found that it is better to focus your energy on the older child, who will be more likely to become upset if told off, hurried or made to feel left out. I always felt that if the baby was washed, dried, warm, fed and in bed he had to make do with the briefest of cuddles at that time of day. With the baby safely in bed it enabled me to concentrate on giving the older child/children a bit of quality time – last story, cuddle, reassurance.

- Try to distract a toddler at this time of day if his behaviour is uncooperative rather than trying to correct him. If, for example, you know that your toddler gets cross if he isn't allowed to help dry the baby, or has a tendency to be less gentle with his new baby brother or sister at bedtime, give him less opportunity to interact. Whisk the baby off to bed and encourage the 'kiss baby brother or sister' behaviour in the morning, when everyone is rested and the older child's behaviour is more predictable.

- Try to get both children upstairs no later than 6pm. It is essential during the early days that the baby does not become overtired. Remember that he will be ready to sleep two hours from the time he last woke. You will also need to take into consideration how long he slept in the late afternoon. If it was only a short nap, I would aim to get him into bed by 6.30pm.

- Whether you attempt to bath both your toddler and your baby together will depend very much on the age of your toddler and how active he tends to be in the bath. The following describes two approaches to dealing with bath time. I suggest that you give both of them a try to decide which one will work best for you.

Bathing the baby and toddler together

In order for this to work you will need to put the baby in one of the specially designed moulded plastic bath seats that he can lie back in and which will free up both your hands. Wash the toddler first, so that he can play while you quickly wash the baby. Have a changing mat on the bathroom floor so that you can transfer the baby to it to be dried, massaged and dressed while you keep an eye on the toddler.

Having been fed at 5pm, the baby should be happy to lie on the changing mat once dressed – long enough for you to get the toddler out of the bath and dried and creamed.

Take both children through to the bedroom and encourage your toddler to dress himself while you give the baby the second breast or the remainder of his bottle feed.

Once the toddler is dressed he should be encouraged to sit next to you to drink his milk while you read him a story or he watches a video.

Try to create a calm quiet atmosphere at this time so that neither child gets over-stimulated or over-excited. Make sure that there are not lots of toys lying around that will encourage your toddler to get hyped up.

Whatever you do, do not tell your toddler that he must not shout or run around because you are trying to get the baby to sleep, as this is the fastest way to ensure that he will start running around screaming at the top of his voice. Instead, explain that it is quiet time now and once the baby is asleep he will have some special time with Mummy.

If your toddler is active and not the type to sit still while you are putting the baby to bed, establish a ritual in which the toddler has a special toy in the baby's room. One idea I found particularly effective was for the toddler to have several little beds (painted boxes, with handmade blankets, etc.) to put his special toys to sleep in, so that when you take the baby through to settle him in his cot, he can bring the special toys through. He can give each toy in turn a drink from their own special bottle or beaker before quietly tucking them in.

A few minutes prior to settling the baby in the cot, make a point of using a low quiet voice to tell baby that he must be very quiet now as it is time to go in his cot so that you can read his big brother a very special story. Emphasise to the baby what a good

THE NEW BABY 159

boy his big brother is and how quiet he is. Of course this must all be done within earshot of the toddler!

Once the baby is settled in his cot you can take the toddler to his room and read him his special story. You will have to be strict about how long you spend reading to him, otherwise a situation will arise where he will want just one more story and the bedtime settling begins to take longer and longer. I suggest that you allow no longer than 15–20 minutes of reading. If he is still resistant about going to sleep, refer to page 163 for how to deal with this problem.

Bathing separately
If bathing both children at the same time is too daunting in the early days, then establish a separate bath time routine for each child. It is advisable to start earlier if you still want both children in bed by 7.30pm, as it will obviously take longer to bath and settle each child separately.

Bring the 5pm feed forward by 15 minutes so that you can then bring the bath time forward for the baby. Get your toddler to help you with bathing, drying and massaging the baby. I always used to encourage the toddler to wash, dry and cream the baby's feet, counting his toes. It will hopefully distract him from the more delicate parts of the baby's body, such as the head, eyes and mouth.

Once the baby is ready to feed, you can adopt the same ritual as described above, but omitting the toddler's milk at this stage. You should manage to settle the baby in his cot by 6.30pm. If he has fed and winded well but does not seem ready to sleep, you can still lay him in his cot, but leave a dim light on and prop a cot mirror or baby cot book along the side for him to look at. I used to have to do this when I was settling twins in the evening and they very quickly got into the habit of going in the cot while wide awake and gazing happily at their books or mirror before drifting off to sleep.

This will allow you to start the toddler's bath at around 6.30pm, aiming to be reading his story and giving him his milk at around 7pm, thus ensuring that he is in bed by 7.15 to 8.15pm.

Q My 18-month-old does not go to nursery for another six months, and I am finding it difficult to take him to his usual morning activities while breast-feeding the baby. Life is becoming very difficult between 9.30am and 12 noon, when I have to try to keep a boisterous toddler occupied for nearly two hours while I am trying to get a very sleepy six-week-old baby to feed. This is leaving me very distressed, anxious and lonely.

A I frequently speak to mothers who are coping completely alone and who do not want to ask for help. However, when you have a new baby this is probably the most important time to call on friends and family – and a time when they will be most willing to lend a hand. Very often grandparents, who can seem reluctant to help out, become the most diligent and useful of resources to call upon. It is usually the case that before being asked to help they stayed away because they didn't want to interfere. Even if they are not able to get directly involved in the childcare, they may be able to help you with the shopping or ironing or other household chores.

Some grandparents will have forgotten how difficult these first few months can be, when you are juggling the demands of a new baby and a toddler, and a gentle reminder may be all that is needed to turn them into a great support. For most mothers this can be a more difficult period than the arrival of the first baby. Relatives tend to be very supportive when it's the first time, but forget that it is the dual demands of a new baby and a toddler that can create the greatest challenge. If you are fortunate enough to have grandparents at hand, do try to organise a regular time each week when they help you, either by taking the toddler to the park or allowing you a little time out with your toddler while they look after the new baby.

The greatest challenge is often the time it takes to breast-feed when you already have a two-year-old. Seeing their mother immobilised on the sofa breast-feeding can bring out the worst in some toddlers. One tip is to try expressing. A new baby will take a bottle more quickly than a breast, and this may enable you to feed the baby more quickly during this time of day. Expressing is also a good way of keeping up your milk supply.

If you do not have grandparents at hand, then look to your friends. Most mothers will rally round and offer to help you with the toddler, take the baby for a walk or simply entertain your toddler while you breast-feed. Do try to be as helpful as possible to your friends before the new baby arrives, since this way you will feel more comfortable asking for help, and your toddler will know your friends better and be more prepared to go to them.

Also find out whether you have a mother and toddler group in your area, and organise to attend this once a week. These groups are inexpensive and the people that go tend to be very supportive. There are usually quite a few around, so try them out and choose the one that suits your needs best. I would encourage you to get out of the house rather than spending all morning inside getting upset and frustrated with your toddler. If you are following the routines for a new-born in *The New Contented Little Baby Book*, you will find that after your baby has had her 10am feed, you have an hour or so to go for a short walk to the park, when ideally your baby will be awake and your toddler will need some exercise. Young children do need the opportunity to go out, and unless the weather is really wet and cold, I always suggest getting a little fresh air in the morning. Toddlers love the rain and, providing they are well wrapped up and the baby is suitably protected, a short outing will always be a good thing. It will enable you to see some other faces – mostly mothers and dog-walkers, to take a bit of exercise and, most importantly, to tire your child for his midday nap and your much needed rest!

Q: I have to take my three-year-old to nursery three mornings a week, and on these days I find that the routine goes totally wrong. As you advise, I put the baby in his buggy around 8.45am, which is the time we leave the house, and he usually drifts off to sleep within five to ten minutes. As it only takes ten minutes to walk to the nursery, I am normally back in the house by 9.15am, at which time the baby will wake up, and refuse to go back to sleep. Although he has had a full feed at 7am, he will not wait until the recommended time of 11am for his next feed. This then has a knock-on effect throughout the rest of the day and puts the whole routine out.

A Instead of heading directly home, why not keep walking? If you can prolong your outing by 20 minutes, your baby will certainly remain asleep. Time it to get home at 9.45am. The motion of being pushed in the pram should have the right effect. Perhaps you could combine this with a walk to the shops to top up on groceries or a stroll to the park. It is so difficult for a mother of two under-three-year-olds to have any time to herself and her own thoughts, and your extended walk will give you the possibility of a little quiet time, while also having the benefit of keeping your baby in the routine.

Q My second baby is nearly seven months old and like my first child has followed the routine really well. However, I am now experiencing a problem in moving his lunch to nearer 12 o'clock as your book recommends. I have to pick my toddler up from nursery at 12 o'clock. This means I have to leave the house at 11.30am. I have tried pushing the baby's lunch to 1pm, when we get back from the nursery run, but he is so tired that he will only eat a small amount before getting irritable and refusing to eat any more. If I try to give him an early lunch at 11am, he is not hungry enough and, again, will only eat a small amount.

He is starting to wake up earlier and earlier in the morning, and I am sure it is because his food intake has dropped during the day.

A This can often be a problem. I usually advise solving it by splitting the baby's lunch. If he is very hungry by 11.30am, I would feed him his savoury food at about 11.15am, before you leave for nursery, and then give him his pudding when you get back from nursery. As your baby becomes bigger, you will find it easier, since it will probably suit you better to feed both the children at the same time, and in another couple of months it is likely that he will be happy to wait until 12.30pm for his lunch, when he can eat with his sibling.

Q My eldest child slept through the night at 10 weeks. I'm doing the same routine with the second – why isn't it working?

A Children are all different and while one may adapt to a routine with ease it may take longer and require more perseverance and patience with a second. It is important not to despair, but take confidence from the aspects of the routine that are working and try not to worry. Stress and anxiety can exhaust you. Your baby will eventually sleep through the night.

Q I'm concerned about my milk supply, which is dropping rapidly. I'm expressing as you suggest, but I can't keep up. Should I try mixed feeding? I always had plenty of milk for my first child.

A Exhaustion is probably the major factor here. With your first child you were able to sleep when he did, but a toddler can prevent this and resting can feel impossible. Introducing a bottle of formula at 10pm can be a lifesaver, as someone else can give your baby this feed while you get to bed early. Not eating enough is another factor. It's hard to do more than grab a snack when you are looking after a toddler and a baby. Try to sit down with your toddler for a proper lunch once the baby has gone down for his midday nap. Make sure you have a supply of bananas and other quick energy foods to keep you going during the day.

Bedtime battles

The toddler who refuses to go to bed is a very common problem and this often coincides with the arrival of a new baby. In my experience, the main reason that this happens is because the mother does not anticipate how much longer everything will take when she is trying to settle two children. What used to be a calm and happy event often begins to resemble a battleground as an exhausted mother tries to cope with both the toddler and the screaming baby. Obviously, once it has got to this stage the baby's needs have to be attended to first, which means the toddler has even more time to become frustrated and overtired. By the time the baby is settled, the toddler has become so overtired that it can take hours to settle him. The key to avoiding this situation is to do a little pre-planning and to start the bedtime routine early.

The following are suggestions on how to plan and prepare a stress-free bedtime for two children, or a toddler who is difficult to settle:

• Try to ensure that your toddler has his main protein meal of the day at lunchtime. This means that tea can be something quick and easy to prepare, such as pasta or a thick soup with sandwiches.
• As the children are waking up from their midday nap, lay out everything that is needed for the bath and bedtime. Towels, cotton wool, flannels, nightwear, nappies, bibs, muslins, etc. should all be put in the places where they are to be used.
• During the afternoon do not allow your toddler to keep taking different toys out of the cupboard if he has not tidied away the ones he has finished with. Encourage him to tidy away all or at least some of his toys.
• Tea should be ready and your toddler seated at 5pm sharp, so that you can sit down and feed the baby at the same time as your toddler is eating his tea.
• Both children should be taken upstairs no later than 5.45pm, to allow plenty of time for the bath and for winding down.
• Try to have both children bathed and dressed by 6.15pm to allow enough time for the baby to take the second half of his feed. Do not allow your toddler to start drinking his milk until you are all settled and ready to watch a video or read a story, while the baby is feeding. Hopefully your toddler will be occupied by the book or video or by drinking his milk long enough to allow you to finish feeding the baby.
• Even if the baby does not look tired, settle him in his cot. Dim the lights and prop a small book or mirror down the side of the cot. If this habit is established early enough, most babies will learn to settle quickly and easily on their own.
• In the early days most babies will be asleep by 6.30–6.45pm, which should allow you enough time to settle the toddler with his night-time story before he becomes overtired.

Sibling rivalry: jealousy

Sibling rivalry is not something new; it has existed since the beginning of time. A new baby represents a threat to the older children, especially first children who have enjoyed the undivided love and attention of their parents. Your child will have to come to terms with the loss of some of your time, which can often lead to him feeling very insecure and behaving in all sorts of ways that you consider to be unreasonable.

Many books and baby magazines give advice on how to prepare a toddler or child for the arrival of a new baby. A lot of emphasis is placed on reading one of the many books especially written for children about the arrival of a new baby. Mothers are also told to encourage their toddler to speak to the baby in the womb and to allow him to help prepare the nursery. This is all good advice, but personally I feel that many unfortunate situations could be avoided by establishing the correct rules and guidelines for the toddler or child well in advance of the arrival of the new baby.

The following scenario explains how clear and firm limits for young toddlers can help to avoid some of the very many difficult situations that so many parents experience when a new baby arrives.

Thomas, aged 15 months, is playing in his parents' bedroom – a ritual that takes place every Sunday morning. Thomas, crawling but not yet walking, has a great fascination with Daddy's tennis and squash balls, which are stored behind a large armchair. He plays happily for 20 minutes or so rolling the balls back and forth to his parents (his mother is three months pregnant), who take this opportunity to lie and relax on the bed while reading the Sunday papers. Occasionally, Thomas manages to aim a ball so it lands on his parents' bed. They gently throw the ball back, stressing the importance of throwing it gently. Both Thomas and his parents get much pleasure out of this little ritual.

However, imagine the scene six months down the line, when the new baby has joined the parents on the bed. Thomas, now 21 months, is walking and much stronger. He is unlikely to be satisfied with just rolling the balls and much more likely to attempt to throw and toss them in the air. The parents' sudden attempts to try to stop the ritual that has gone on for many months only leads to Thomas getting very upset. Their repeated warnings to Thomas to be careful when he is rolling the balls have no effect, and the inevitable happens – the baby gets hit by a flying ball, resulting in screams all round. The shocked and worried parents, while trying to console the crying baby, lose their temper with Thomas (who is now also screaming), calling him 'naughty' and 'careless'.

Whether Thomas threw the ball at the baby on purpose we will never know, and it is not the issue of the story. The issue is whether he should ever have been allowed to play with the balls in the bedroom in the first place. To me this is a typical example of unclear limits being set for a child. It was ridiculous ever to expect the child to be satisfied with throwing the ball gently – balls are not designed for gentle play. Therefore the parents' expectation of Thomas – that he would play gently with the ball in the bedroom – was unrealistic. This is a case of the different limits for outside play and inside play not being set properly.

When deciding on rules and limits for toddlers, parents would do well to think in advance of the time when a new baby will arrive and whether the rules and limits they are setting now will be realistic then.

How to breast-feed and cope with a toddler

I am frequently asked by exasperated mothers how they should deal with their toddler while they are breast-feeding their baby. This is undoubtedly one of the most difficult times for a mother to cope, and it is also one that it is crucially important to get right from the beginning. The following scenario shows how the peaceful afternoon of mother, baby and toddler can rapidly disintegrate into an all-out screaming match. It should help you to identify ways of avoiding such problems occurring in the first place.

Rachel (the mother), Alexander (aged 23 months) and baby William (aged four weeks) are all in the sitting room. Baby William is just finishing off his breast-feed, which takes about 35 minutes. During this time Alexander behaves perfectly, playing with his toys and chatting happily to his mother. His mother makes a particular point of repeatedly telling Alexander what a good boy he is and how much his baby brother loves him. She constantly encourages Alexander to stroke the baby's head, impressing the importance of being very gentle and loving with William.

RACHEL: Alexander, why don't you tidy away your toys while Mummy changes William?

She lays William on his changing mat on the floor while she gets the changing things.

ALEXANDER: No, don't want.

RACHEL: If you put your toys away quickly, Mummy will give you a nice biscuit.

Alexander then starts to whinge and stamp his feet as he proceeds to throw his toys across the room, aiming for the toy box. The commotion sets the baby off crying, and Rachel begins to get fraught.

RACHEL: Alexander, be careful putting your toys away. One may accidentally hit your brother and hurt him.

Alexander promptly throws a small ball at his baby brother, hitting him on the head. The baby screams with fright, and the mother screams at Alexander.

RACHEL: You bad boy! You're very naughty. You've made poor baby William cry. If you ever do that again I will take all your toys away, and there will be no more biscuits.

Alexander starts screaming and throwing his toys everywhere.

ALEXANDER: Don't want toys; don't want biscuit; no baby, no Mummy.

Rachel then attempts to calm the situation down. She cuddles the sobbing Alexander and gives him the biscuit, which he was promised if he had put his toys away nicely. She explains how much she loves him and that she knows he is really a good little boy and that good little boys must not throw their toys around and be nasty to people.

Within minutes a happy family scene has turned into an uncontrollable situation of anger, jealousy, whingeing, bribery, threats, fear and frustration. Alexander at this stage doesn't really care whether he is called good, bad or naughty, because he is now getting what he wanted all along: love, cuddles and attention from Mummy.

If we go through the whole scenario again step by step we can see what prompted Alexander's behaviour and the way in which one can avoid, or at least minimise, potential problems in this type of situation.

Rachel, aware that the baby's feed would take at least 30–40 minutes, was anxious that Alexander should remain calm and happy throughout the feed. She settled him with his toys and from the start gave Alexander lots of praise. Modern-day psychology places great emphasis on praising good behaviour and ignoring bad, and getting the toddler involved with the new baby from the outset. In theory this seems sound advice, but unfortunately all too often, as in Alexander's case, it backfires. While Alexander appeared to be happy and content playing with his toys while his mother fed the baby, I am sure that after 15–20 minutes his boredom was growing. He was more than likely not feeling like the good boy his mother kept insisting he was, and fed up with constantly having to admire the baby.

By the time the feed was coming to an end he was feeling very bored and frustrated and he wanted some individual attention from his mother. Having to clear away his toys and wait until his mother had changed the baby's nappy to get a cuddle and a biscuit probably seemed too much.

He wanted things to be how they were before the baby came along – for Mummy to be there when he needed her and not to have to share her with this very demanding other person. In his eyes, if the baby could scream and get his mother's immediate attention, then that is the way he would get it as well. At 23 months of age and with a new baby brother, he was experiencing many new emotions. When placed in a situation where several of these emotions surfaced at the same time, he dealt with this in the only way he knew. The feeding of a young baby can take anything up to one hour, which is a long time for a child of Alexander's age.

The following guidelines explain how to cope with occupying a toddler and feeding a new baby at the same time, hopefully avoiding a temper tantrum:

- At the beginning of the feed Alexander was perfectly happy. At that stage Rachel would have been better advised to get on with feeding the baby and not draw attention to him.
- It would have been better to let Alexander decide for himself if he wanted to admire and talk to the baby.

- Rachel would have done better to change the baby's nappy midway through the feed. By saying, 'Let's go and get some water for William's nappy change and a biscuit and some juice for you', she could have distracted Alexander enough to prevent him from getting bored near the end of the feed.
- Once the baby had finished feeding and with the nappy already changed, Rachel could have put the baby straight into his chair, knowing that all his needs had been met: holding and cuddling, feeding and changing. She would then have been able to give some much needed and undivided attention to Alexander, while making a game of the two of them clearing the toys away.
- It is pointless trying to reason with a distraught toddler about why he should love his baby brother. At this point he is too emotional. The only rule that should have been made clear is that no matter how he feels towards his brother, he is without question never allowed to hurt him.
- Toy chests and baskets are always a potential danger. Different toys should be stored in different boxes, preferably with securely fitting lids, and kept in a cupboard with a door that shuts. This way the mother can ensure that only safe toys are brought out when the baby is around.
- Balls should never be allowed in the house; children should learn from the very earliest age that certain toys and games are for outside play only. This avoids situations like the one I have just described when a second baby arrives.
- The word 'if' is best avoided with small children, as it usually results in parents trying to bribe the child into good behaviour. The child soon begins to believe that the only reason for good behaviour is the reward at the end of it.

7
Habits – the Good, the Bad and the Ugly

While much of this book focuses on establishing good feeding and sleeping habits for babies and toddlers, there are other good habits that can be learned from an early age. Teeth cleaning and hand washing are two that spring to mind. If introduced correctly and in a positive manner at a young age, many battles can be avoided at a later date.

There are also some habits formed in the early days that are considered good at the time but at a later stage are looked upon as bad. For example, most mothers give a sigh of relief when their young baby eventually finds his thumb, and many mothers actively encourage the habit by pushing the baby's thumb into his mouth. Thumb sucking can be an excellent source of comfort and a way for the baby to resettle himself to sleep should he wake in the night or very early morning. But if the child is still sucking his thumb three years down the line, it is a different story. Parents get annoyed and often embarrassed if the child constantly has his thumb in his mouth, especially in public.

Some children become very attached to a blanket, muslin or soft toy. The special comforter, like thumb sucking, is often used to help the baby or child get to sleep by himself or to calm him during times of distress. However, it can turn into a problem if the child becomes obsessive about it and insists on dragging the comforter everywhere.

Nose picking is another common habit that many parents find extremely irritating, and the way some children dispose of the contents can leave even the most liberal parents feeling totally revolted. While the majority of these habits disappear with age, the following guidelines suggest how to prevent bad habits from forming, modify existing ones and encourage good habits. With children over 18 months I find the use of a star chart invaluable. It can be a great incentive to help establish good habits. For the star chart to be effective it is important that there are enough tasks on the chart for the child to achieve some stars every day.

Comforters

Between six and nine months nearly all babies begin to develop an attachment to a comforter. The choice of comforter varies from baby to baby. Some become dependent on a blanket or muslin, others may choose a soft toy or use their thumb or a dummy. Psychologists believe attachment to a comforter occurs around the same age that babies realise they are an individual person, separate from their mother. These transitional comfort objects give a baby or toddler a sense of security when they feel alone or vulnerable. Baby and childcare expert Penelope Leach says that a cuddly toy is thought to be a stand-in for the mother, which the baby or child can use when the mother's comfort is not available to him.

The majority of experts agree that use of a comforter is a normal part of a baby's development, but most stress the importance of a child not becoming over-dependent on it. This can easily be avoided if comforters are restricted to rest times and sleep times. Allowing a baby to drag a muslin, blanket, toy or dummy around everywhere can also lead to disaster if the item in question gets lost.

By three years of age most children have become less reliant on their comforter and the majority will have abandoned it altogether by the time they reach five years.

The following guidelines will help to avoid over-dependency on a comforter, which can lead to problems later on:

- When you notice your baby or toddler becoming attached to a certain object, limit its use to bedtime or special rest time in the house. Do not allow him to drag it from room to room or on trips out – though obviously you will need to take it on holiday or for overnight visits. Otherwise be insistent that the blanket, muslin, toy or dummy stays in the cot.
- If possible, try to purchase a duplicate, as this will allow frequent washing and provide you with a replacement if the item becomes damaged or lost.

- If you find that your young baby or toddler is getting more and more dependent on a comforter and has become withdrawn, not interacting in the way that he used to, there could be some underlying emotional problem. Speak to your health visitor for advice.

Thumb sucking

All babies are born with a basic instinct to suck, and nearly all babies will suck their thumb at some stage. Many start while in the womb, but it is not until a baby reaches almost three months that he will have sufficient hand-to-mouth coordination to keep his thumb in his mouth for any length of time. Once the baby has developed the necessary coordination for thumb sucking, how often he will do it and for how long varies considerably from baby to baby. The majority of young babies who suck their thumb do so when tired, when using the thumb as a comforter prior to sleep or when hungry. Thumb sucking or hand chewing usually peaks between the ages of six and nine months, with the need to suck gradually decreasing by the age of one year. While some babies continue to suck their thumb at bedtime, a baby who is continually sucking his thumb throughout the day is more likely to develop a long-term habit that will be difficult to break.

If your baby is approaching a year old and is constantly sucking his thumb during the day, the cause is probably boredom. The best way to deal with this is to encourage more physical activity such as Tumble Tots or a swimming class. When at home, encourage more crawling or pushing of his baby walker and remember to rotate his toys so that he doesn't get bored. At a year old, babies are learning how to entertain themselves and need encouragement from their parents or carers towards this aim. Games such as shape sorters and rings are good for encouraging toddlers to use their fingers. I believe that distraction is much better than disapproval. Making a fuss about thumb sucking or constantly pulling his thumb out of his mouth rarely works and usually makes the baby or toddler more anxious, which increases his need to suck.

With older children excessive sucking may become a real problem as it can cause deformities of the teeth and jaw, resulting in the need for extensive dental treatment. Again, disapproval of the habit rarely works; it is much better to work out the cause. Boredom, tiredness and insecurity are usually the main reasons. I often find that suggesting to an older child that he is tired and perhaps should go and have a rest in his room where he can suck his thumb in private immediately encourages him to find something better to do.

Dummies

If your baby reaches one year and is still dependent on his dummy, particularly to get to sleep, it would be wise to try to break the habit during the second year. The older he gets, the harder it will be for him to give it up. Apart from the possible damage that the constant sucking on a dummy can do to his teeth, you should also consider the social implications. Toddlers and older children often become targets of ridicule by their peers if they are known still to use a dummy.

If you are planning to eliminate the dummy, the following points should be considered:

- Do not allow relatives or friends to make fun of your child for still using a dummy. In my experience, comments such as, 'Only babies have dummies' or 'You look silly with that dreadful thing in your mouth' can make a sensitive child feel very inferior, causing him much stress and increasing his need for the dummy.
- Never attempt to get rid of the dummy just prior to or straight after the arrival of a new baby.
- Your toddler or child should be in good health and fully recovered from any illness when you attempt to wean him off his dummy.
- Eliminating the dummy should be avoided during times when major changes are about to take place, for example moving house, starting nursery, mother returning to work.
- With an older child who is being stubborn about giving up the dummy, reassure him that you will not take his dummy away from him, but he must use it only in his bedroom. And remind him how proud you will be when he decides to give it to the little babies in the hospital or Aunty Susan's new baby.

How you get rid of the dummy depends very much on the age of your child and how often he uses it. With a toddler aged less than two years it is better to go cold turkey, as he is still too young to reason with. Trying to eliminate gradually rarely works as the constant whingeing and crying over several hours usually wears the parent down into submission. If your toddler is used to having a dummy during the day as well as at night, I would advise that you get rid of it over a weekend when your partner is around. This way you will have help in keeping your toddler very busy with lots activities. He will most probably be miserable for the first day that he is denied it, but getting him out of the house doing things that require lots of physical energy will help to minimise the whingeing. Take him swimming and to the park to play with a ball and go on the swings, roundabout etc. When at home try to involve him with finger painting, gardening and water play. It is also probably better not to attempt to put him in his cot for his midday nap, as it is unlikely he will settle without his dummy, and you do not want to get him worked up into a state in the middle of the day. If you are out and about, he will hopefully have a catnap in the buggy or car.

That evening when you settle him to sleep you can try introducing a special new toy that he will hopefully use as a replacement comforter. He will more than likely be very difficult to settle and you will probably have to do 'controlled crying', checking him every five to ten minutes until he eventually gets to sleep. The same approach should be used in the night if he awakes crying for his dummy. In my experience and from the feedback I get from parents of children this age, the worst is usually over within two to three nights. It is also important to remember when doing controlled crying that you must gradually increase the intervals between checking times, otherwise your toddler will come to depend on you going in every 10 minutes until he falls asleep. I usually advise starting off checking at five-to-ten-minute intervals on the first night and increasing the gap to 10 to 20 minutes on the second night, then by a further 10 minutes on subsequent nights until he is sleeping through. Once he settles quickly at bedtime without the dummy, you may want to try waiting 20 minutes or so before going to him in the night, particularly if the crying is intermittent. It is very possible that he may settle himself back without you having to go in.

With a child over two years one has to be much more careful how getting rid of the dummy is approached. The mind and imagination of a child this age are developing very rapidly, and taking the dummy away suddenly could cause much more emotional upset than it would with a younger child.

If your child is still using the dummy during the day, restrict it to being used in his room. Gradually decreasing his dependency on it will make it easier for you to persuade him to give it up. My cousin persuaded her little girl of three years to give all her dummies to the tiny babies who were in hospital 'and didn't have a dummy'. For being so thoughtful to these little babies she was allowed to choose a special new toy. Simba the lion was a great hit, and helped her to settle to sleep happily at night without the dummy. Another good idea is to get a friend to come around and explain that all the shops have sold out of dummies and her little baby really needs one. Making a nice gesture of wrapping the dummy up in pretty paper to give to the baby as a present often makes an older child feel important about the kind gesture he is making.

Sometimes forgetting to pack the dummy when you go on holiday will also work. The fact that children are normally so excited about going on holiday, and bedtimes are usually much later with no pressure of work for parents during the day, can help get over the first couple of days of the dummy being eliminated. Trips to the beach and extra treats of an ice cream for being such a good boy or girl managing without their dummy will also help make the first couple of days go more smoothly.

Nail biting

Nail biting should be treated in much the same way as thumb sucking. It is better to distract the child than to reprimand him. If a child's nail biting is caused by anxiety, making a fuss about the habit will only make him more anxious and inclined to bite his nails more. Finding out what is causing his anxiety and resolving the problem will often help eliminate the habit.

For the majority of children, nail biting is nothing more than a habit they will eventually outgrow. Some parents try painting their children's fingernails with a bitter-tasting solution, but I have never known this approach to be very successful.

I have had some degree of success using a star chart. The child is encouraged to give up biting one nail at a time, and for each day that he doesn't bite that particular nail, he gets a star. It is important that no mention is made of the other nails he has bitten. At the end of the week, depending on how many stars he has on the chart, he will get a small present. If he has managed to go one week without biting that particular nail, encourage him to give up biting a second nail. This very gradual approach can take a while, but it does put less pressure on the child. Often the appearance of a few unbitten nails is enough encouragement for some children to give up the habit completely. It is important to file any rough edges regularly and to emphasise how nice his unbitten nails look.

I also find that encouraging a toddler to massage his hands regularly with cream can be an incentive to take pride in them.

Dawdling

Dawdling is very common between the ages of two and three. It also coincides with the age when many toddlers start nursery. All too often I have witnessed the scene of fraught parents struggling to get their toddler fed, washed and dressed in time for school. The more the parents coax and cajole him to hurry up, the more he dawdles. To avoid this habit turning mornings into a war zone it is important to set strict rules for the morning routine. Ideally, the pattern should be established long before the toddler starts nursery.

The first thing that must happen when your toddler awakes is that he gets washed and dressed. He should then immediately be given breakfast. Once breakfast is over he should be encouraged to get everything ready that he needs to take to school. As an incentive, tell him that once he has done all these things he will be allowed 15 minutes to play, read a book or watch a video.

It is essential that you are consistent and firm so that he learns what is expected of him in the morning. This is all part of teaching a toddler to take responsibility for himself. The star chart is also a great way to help enforce this behaviour

Tidiness

Getting your toddler into the habit of tidying up from an early age will help to avoid much conflict at a later stage. Toddlers can be encouraged to keep their toys and clothes tidy as soon as they are able to walk. They should also learn that they have to tidy one set of toys away before getting another set out. This is easier to implement if toys are stored in different categories, in boxes with secure lids. This storage system also helps the toddler to define size, shape and colour. The cars belong in the long red box, the jigsaws belong in the tall green box and the crayons belong in the small round yellow box. While a large toy chest may be attractive to look at, I feel it is best avoided as it will do little to encourage tidiness.

Rocking and head banging

Between six and twelve months some babies get into the habit of getting up on all fours and rocking their head back and forth. Others lie on their back and roll their head from side to side. This usually happens when they are tired or about to go to sleep. Occasionally a baby may even bang his head continuously against the cot spars until he falls asleep. This rhythmic behaviour can be very upsetting for parents because it is often associated with children who are emotionally disturbed.

If your baby displays this behaviour only when he is tired and ready to go to sleep, there is very little to worry about. He is using these rhythmic movements to comfort himself. However, if he appears unhappy and fretful and displays this behaviour when awake, it is advisable to seek advice from your doctor or health visitor.

Nose picking

Many of the childcare books I have read say that nose picking is often done out of boredom or when the child is stressed. While this may be the case with some children, I believe the main reason is that the majority of children are not capable of blowing their nose until they reach three to four years of age. It is inevitable that a toddler will clear his nose of any irritating mucus the only way he can – by picking it.

Once your toddler reaches two or three years of age you can help him to learn how to blow his nose by demonstrating how to close one nostril while blowing down the other.

Like the majority of annoying habits, nose picking disappears with time. It is pointless reprimanding the child for picking his nose, but he should be reminded that it is something he should do in private.

Stammering

Stammering is very common between the ages of two and three years. It is also around this age that a toddler's vocabulary rapidly increases, to 200 words or more. Therefore it is hardly surprising that a great many toddlers experience difficulty in articulating some words. Avoid becoming obsessed with your child's pronunciation by constantly making him repeat words correctly. In my experience, a toddler who becomes anxious and tense will be more likely to stutter or stammer. The majority of children will lose the habit of stammering by the time they reach four or five years, but if you have serious concerns about your child's speech development, you should discuss them with your doctor or health visitor.

Whingeing

All toddlers go through stages of being whiney. I have found that toddlers who were fussy and demanding as babies and never learned to entertain themselves are more inclined to develop a habit of whingeing. If you think your toddler's whingeing is becoming a serious habit, it is advisable to deal with it sooner rather than later. A child who is constantly whingeing and demanding will soon become very unpopular. The most effective way of dealing with a child who is whingeing is to sit him down and in a very serious manner explain that you cannot understand what he is saying when he speaks in a whiney voice. Tell him he must speak properly if he wants you to listen.

Thereafter when he whinges, say very simply and very firmly, 'I can't hear you', then walk away. It is imperative not to become involved in any sort of conversation whatsoever until he speaks properly. The reason he is whingeing in the first place is to get your attention. If he learns that you will totally ignore any whingeing he will soon stop.

Private parts

Many parents get very concerned when their baby or toddler begins to explore and play with his private parts. A young baby will discover his genitals in much the same way that he does his mouth, hands and feet, and many babies derive some pleasure from rubbing them. This behaviour was more noticeable when babies used to sleep on their tummies. I have observed babies as young as six weeks vigorously rocking and rubbing themselves in a rhythmical movement against the mattress. The pleasure that this action brings a young baby is self-comforting and not at all sexual. If your baby develops this totally normal and unconscious habit, it is best just to ignore it.

Once a toddler is out of nappies the interest in his genitals becomes more obvious. If your toddler gets into a habit of playing with his private parts, it is important that you do not scold him or make him feel bad about his body. However, it is advisable to teach him that some things are best done in private.

Teeth cleaning

Until your child has several teeth it will probably be easier to clean his teeth using the specially designed gauze pads that are currently available. These pads will enable you to rub his teeth and gums gently, removing any plaque and keeping his mouth free of bacteria.

Once he has several teeth you can use a small milk-teeth toothbrush. Choose one that has soft-ended bristles and a chunky ribbed handle, making it easier for your baby or toddler to hold. To begin with, most babies and toddlers are more interested in chewing the brush than in actually brushing their teeth. It is not until a child reaches six or seven years that he will begin to clean his teeth properly; until then he will need your help. Try to make cleaning his teeth fun. Play a game of Mummy's turn, your turn. With children under three it is usually easier to clean their teeth just before they get out of the bath, which avoids having to worry about dribbling. If your child is still having milk after the bath, it is a good idea to give his teeth another quick clean after his milk, when he is in bed. I usually do this with a tiny amount of toothpaste, a wet toothbrush and a tissue for dribbles.

The following guidelines will ensure that you establish the right habits for healthy teeth:

- It is important to use toothpaste that contains the correct level of fluoride for milk teeth and is sugar-free. Using toothpaste that contains too much fluoride can result in white specks on permanent teeth. A small pea-sized blob of toothpaste is all that is needed.
- Ensure that your child's teeth are brushed at least twice a day. This will ensure that they are protected by the fluoride, which stays in the mouth up to five hours after brushing.
- Always ensure that the toothbrush is rinsed thoroughly after each use and that it is stood upright to dry. It should be replaced every two months.
- Fresh fruit juice diluted with water should be given with meals, not between meals. Acidic juices can damage the soft surface of children's teeth, so choose non-acidic ones. By the time a child reaches a year old he should be having all drinks from a cup or beaker.
- Babies who are still being settled at bedtime with a bottle of milk are more likely to suffer from tooth decay, which can affect permanent teeth that have not yet come through.
- Get your toddler used to visiting the dentist before he reaches 18 months. The younger he is when he visits, the less likely he is to feel intimidated. Try to choose a practice that specialises in children's dentistry.
- Once a toddler reaches the dawdling stage it is worthwhile investing in a Toothbrush Timer Set. This comprises a junior toothbrush and novelty stand that incorporates a timer. Rewarding the child with a star if he finishes brushing his teeth within the allocated time can be a great incentive.

Cleaning hands and nails

Once your baby starts on solids you should get into the habit of washing his hands before and after meals. When he starts walking you can begin teaching him how to wash his hands at the sink. By the time they reach two-and-a-half the majority of children are capable of washing their hands by themselves, although they will need supervision when filling the sink and help with drying their hands properly. Never leave your toddler unsupervised if he is able to turn on the hot water tap by himself.

To encourage good hand washing habits, fill a small plastic container with novelty soaps, nail brushes and animal-shape painting sponges. Most children find it more fun to soap the novelty sponge or nailbrush, and then wash their hands with it. Drying hands will be made easier for the toddler if he uses a facecloth rather than a towel. Choose one with his favourite cartoon character on it and hang it on a small hook at a height that makes it easy for him to reach.

Hands should be washed before and after meals and after a visit to the loo. They should also be washed on return from an outing or from playing outside and after handling pets.

It is also important to keep your baby or toddler's fingernails short and clean. This is easy with very young babies, as nails can be cut when they are asleep. With toddlers it can be more difficult, as most hate having their nails cut. I usually find they are less likely to protest if allowed to watch a video while their nails are cut. I'm afraid this is the one time I usually resort to bribery!

Hair washing

A great many of the toddlers I know hate having their hair washed and will scream blue murder throughout the process. There is a specially designed shampoo shield that you can put on the child's head to reduce the chances of water getting in their eyes, but the majority of parents who have purchased this tell me that it makes little or no difference to the child's screaming. The best advice seems to be to ignore the screams and forge ahead as quickly as possible. The sooner hair washing is finished, the sooner the screaming will stop.

Q My three-year-old daughter used to be perfectly happy to go to the hairdresser's and have her hair cut. Now she screams the place down the minute she is put in the chair.

My hairdresser is very patient, but what used to take 15 minutes can now take 30 or 40 minutes, and I am getting more and more stressed and embarrassed each time I have to take her.

A Many young children have a fear of the hairdresser's and I always advise parents whenever possible not to force the issue of taking a young child to have his hair cut if he is very frightened. If you are not confident about trimming your daughter's hair yourself, there are many hairdressers who provide a home visit service. As your daughter is not at the age yet to need a designer haircut, I would advise that you find someone who will come to the house. That way you can sit her on your knee or allow her to watch her favourite video while her hair is being trimmed. It can also be a good idea to get two or three of your friends to come round with their kids and have a hair-trimming party.

It may also help to buy your daughter a toy hairdressing kit and play hairdresser's with her. My mother always used to let me brush and comb her hair and gave me lots of compliments on my styling. She also made a big fuss about how beautiful my own hair looked when it was washed and dried, which encouraged me to enjoy my trips to the hairdresser's from a very young age.

8
Playing It Safe

The majority of babies begin to take their first steps just before their first birthday. These steps signify the beginning of a baby's journey into toddlerhood. Once he is walking, his perception of the world around him suddenly changes and his curiosity increases, as he views things from an upright level. This newfound mobility is a vital stage in your child's development, giving him the independence to explore his surroundings and the ability to learn other skills.

During this stage of development it is essential that a toddler has a safe, happy and relaxed environment to master these skills confidently. Toddlers soon become very frustrated if they keep hearing the word 'no' or are constantly reminded to be careful or not to touch. In my experience, much conflict and many tears and tantrums can be avoided if parents create a home that allows their toddler to grow up freely and safely.

Usually, I can tell very quickly which of my babies will experience more difficulties during their toddler years. I must confess that my prediction, which nearly always turns out to be accurate, has rarely been based on the character of the baby. My analysis is usually based on the character of the parents and drawn from my experience of living in the home that they have created.

I am not suggesting that the home should be turned into a mini version of Disneyland, but it is essential to 'toddlerproof' it and move anything hazardous out of reach. There should also be at least one room in the house where the toddler is able to play and explore happily and freely without the risk of hurting himself. It is important that his natural curiosity is not hampered by being constantly nagged to be careful with Mummy's precious china plant-pot holder, or not to get dirty finger marks on the lovely white paintwork.

Childproofing your home

No doubt you will already have childproofed your home to some extent when your baby started to crawl, but as he enters toddler-hood and becomes more physically and mentally independent, his desire to explore increases rapidly. Toddlers are naturally inquisitive, as this is how they learn about the world around them, and every day brings a whole new range of challenges and experiences. During the first year parents can put their baby in a playpen or cot or strap them into a baby-seat or swing for a short period, knowing that they are safe and unable to come to any harm. During the second year this is not the case. Once the toddler becomes mobile, he quickly learns how to climb out of the playpen or cot or undo the safety straps of his buggy or chair. A home that was safe for your baby may be a potential minefield for your toddler. It is advisable to review how childproof your home really is and whether all the necessary gadgets for home safety are in place. Even then it is important to remember that accidents are the most common cause of fatality for children between the ages of one and four. Every week three fatal injuries occur as a result of accidents in the home and thousands of children are seriously injured, so constant supervision is crucial during this stage.

High risk areas

The rooms where your toddler spends most of his time are where the majority of accidents tend to happen, namely the kitchen and the sitting room. In all of these rooms you should have the doors fitted with door-slam protectors to prevent your toddler from trapping his fingers, and glass doors should be fitted with safety-proof film. Radiators should be kept on a low temperature so that your toddler does not burn himself should he touch them. All windows should be fitted with safety locks that allow the window to be opened slightly but not far enough for your toddler to squeeze out. Check furniture for sharp corners and if necessary fit safety covers. Chairs should not be positioned in places that could give your toddler access to potentially dangerous spots in the room. All electrical sockets should be covered with safety covers, and cables and electrical leads should be out of reach. Lamps placed on small tables covered with table covers are a particular safety hazard, as a toddler who is just learning to walk could grab on to the table cover for support if he loses his balance. All low cupboards, drawers and the fridge/freezer should be fitted with childproof catches. Ensure that dishwashers, washing machines and tumble-dryers are switched off at the mains when not in use and that their doors are kept closed at all times.

Perfume, aftershave, medicines, chemicals, household cleaning materials and batteries should be locked away or out of reach at all times. Buttons, beads, plastic bags, coins, pens, pencils, drawing pins, paper-clips and other small objects are just a few of the things that are potentially dangerous if swallowed by your toddler, so make sure they are stored safely out of his reach.

In order not to hamper your toddler's natural curiosity and desire to explore, it is a good idea to set aside one accessible drawer or cupboard in the kitchen and sitting room where you can store and rotate different things that your toddler can play with.

Hallway

The staircase can be another potential danger and accounts for most accidents. Install a proper child safety gate at the top and bottom of the stairs and always check that nothing has been dropped on the stairs before going up or down them. Never try to carry your toddler up the stairs in one arm and something else in the other. Toddlers are very wriggly as well as unpredictable, so always keep one hand on the banister to support yourself. Once your toddler is capable of going up the stairs himself, teach him how to come back down safely, either step by step on his bottom or feet first on his tummy. Never allow him to go up- or downstairs unsupervised and teach him not to turn around on the stairs or look back when going up them, in case he loses his balance. Do not leave balls and toys, trikes and skateboards lying about in the hallway, and ensure that items such as umbrellas, walking sticks and golf clubs are not accessible.

Bathroom

Never leave your toddler in the bath alone, not even for a few seconds. If you have forgotten the towel, it is better to lift your toddler out of the bath wet, wriggling and possibly screaming than risk the possibility of a serious accident occurring.

Toddlers have been known to drown in the shallowest of water and even when secured in one of the chairs designed for the bath. It is also important that you place a non-slip mat in the bottom of the bath and cover the taps with a safety shield. Even then, do not let your toddler stand up or jump around in the bath. Fit a childproof lock on the lid of the loo seat to prevent him from lifting it and getting his fingers jammed, or even falling into the loo.

Remove all medicines and cleaning fluids from the bathroom, and ensure that bubble bath, lotions and talcum powder are out of reach or in a secure cupboard.

The nursery

Once your toddler transfers from a cot to a bed it is particularly important to ensure that his room is a totally safe place to be, especially because most of the time he spends there will be on his own.

It is advisable to continue to use a baby listener to monitor your toddler until he is at least three years of age. Even with window locks fitted, his cot or bed should be placed well away from the window. It should also be away from radiators. I have read of one young toddler who died when he fell out of bed and got jammed between his bed and a warm radiator.

Check that all bedroom furniture and bedding is flameproof and that there are no trailing electrical flexes or table lamps in the room. Chests of drawers and bookcases can also be a hazard if the toddler attempts to climb up on to them and they tip forwards. They should be secured to the wall and drawers or cupboards fitted with safety locks so that climbing can be prevented.

High chairs

Always use the safety harness on your toddler's high chair and in addition attach a second set of straps so that he is secured into the chair twice. When your toddler is not in the high chair it is important to ensure that the safety harness is not left dangling. Although it may seem unlikely, tragic accidents have occurred in just such a situation. Never ever leave your toddler unsupervised while in his high chair, particularly when eating. One mother I know left the room for just a couple of minutes and when she got back her toddler was hanging over the side of the chair, gasping for breath and choking on a mouthful of food. It appeared that he had dropped his spoon and was trying to bend over to reach it while his mouth was full. Care should also be taken with certain foods. Grapes, cherry tomatoes, sweets and some small pieces of dried fruit are potentially dangerous if given whole. Toddlers are very prone to over-filling their mouth and trying to swallow without chewing. It is important that you teach your toddler to take small amounts at a time and chew properly before swallowing. This is why eating with your toddler is very important, as these are things that he can learn by role-play. Finally, never allow your toddler to walk or run around while eating or drinking. There could be serious consequences if he trips and falls while drinking from a beaker or eating food.

Cooking and cleaning

If you have to use the front rings of the stove when cooking, make sure that the pan handles are turned away from the front or edge of the cooker. If you have a low level oven, make sure that your toddler does not go near it until it has cooled down after cooking. When stacking the dishwasher ensure that all knives and sharp-edged utensils are placed downwards in the dishwasher and the door always remains firmly closed. When not in use they should always be stored in a place where it is impossible for your toddler to get them.

Do not leave buckets, bowls or containers standing around. Empty them immediately. A toddler can drown in even the shallowest of water. Try to avoid ironing when your toddler is around, and when you do iron make sure that the iron is put well out of reach until it cools down.

Toys and play equipment

Choose toys and equipment that are appropriate for your toddler's age and that he can play with or control safely. Buy good quality brand names that meet British standards. Check the labels to ensure that they contain no small parts that could be dangerous for toddlers. Broken hard toys are a potential danger, as are worn soft toys. Do regular toy and equipment checks and either mend or discard any that are not safe.

Toys are best stored in cupboards or toy boxes with lids as opposed to easy-to-open toy chests or baskets, as this prevents a toddler from pulling out masses of toys and strewing them all around the room. He should be encouraged to play with one or two toys at a time and taught to put them away before he takes any more out. This will help to prevent the possibility of your toddler or someone else tripping over and injuring themselves. When your toddler is playing with younger babies or older children, special caution should be used and they should be supervised at all times. A toy suitable for a three-year-old could be potentially dangerous for a baby. Emphasise the difference between outside and inside play and do not allow your toddler to throw balls in the house or run around clutching items such as crayons, pencils and paintbrushes.

Fire prevention

Fire in the home is one of the main causes of accidental death of young children. Fitting a smoke alarm that conforms to British Safety Standards both upstairs and downstairs is crucial, as is checking the batteries regularly. It is also a good idea to have a safety blanket and small fire extinguisher in the kitchen.

Ensure that all lighting is fitted with the correct wattage of bulb. Ceiling lights and table lamps with shades are a risk if fitted with too strong a bulb. Check all plugs and close all the downstairs doors on going to bed.

Cords and strings

Kettles, irons and telephone cords are all potentially dangerous as are strings, ribbons and cords on curtains and mobiles. Fancy tassels and tiebacks can also present a risk. I won't repeat the tragic real-life incidents I have heard told, but please be aware that fatal accidents happen and it is best to remove or make safe all items that pose a possible threat of injury to your child. Always remove any cot mobile when your baby is asleep in his cot, and once he begins to move around stop using it altogether.

Heating

Central heating radiators that are uncovered should be kept at a temperature that would not burn your toddler should he touch them. It is well worth investing in individual thermostatic controls, so that each room can be controlled to suit your toddler's needs. Electric, gas and coal fires should always be surrounded by a nursery fireguard that can be secured safely to the wall. Freestanding heaters should bear a BEAB mark and always be fitted with a thermostatic control, and automatically cut off if they fall over. They should be positioned away from furniture, in particular soft furnishings and upholstery, and never be used to dry or air clothes. Ideally, they should not be used in a toddler's bedroom, but if this is necessary, they should be turned off and unplugged when the toddler is in the room alone. Remember also to refit the safety cover to the socket when you unplug any electrical equipment and to keep the safety cover in a safe place when not in use.

Lighting

Avoid table lamps in your toddler's bedroom, as the trailing flex is another safety hazard. Fit a dimmer switch to the ceiling light so the brightness can be adjusted, and use a small plug-in socket light that cannot be pulled out by your toddler if he needs to have a night-light on. Alternatively, buy a baby monitor that incorporates a small night-light. Be sure to place the monitor out of reach, with the flex safely behind a chest of drawers or other solid piece of furniture.

Garden

A garden is a wonderful place in which your child can play and run around, getting fresh air while using up his massive amounts of physical energy. No matter how small, it can be made an interesting place for him to explore and learn about outdoor life and nature. It is important that all fences and gates are secure and that there are no gaps in hedges that he can crawl through. Ponds are one of the biggest dangers for young toddlers and should be covered and fenced off, or better still drained of water until your toddler is much older. Garden sheds and garages storing chemicals, DIY tools and equipment should be securely locked and the keys kept in a safe place.

If you have pets, it is important that they are not allowed to foul parts of the garden where your toddler plays, and a close eye should be kept on any neighbouring cats to make sure they are not fouling your garden. Check that your toddler does not have access to any poisonous plants and flowers.

Swings, slides and climbing frames should be secured firmly to the ground and safety matting laid down to prevent serious injuries if your toddler falls. Sandpits should always be kept covered when not in use and checked regularly to make sure that they are free from dirt and debris.

Car safety

Your toddler should always be strapped securely into a properly fitted safety seat while travelling in the car. Never be persuaded to allow your toddler to be held by anyone, no matter how short the journey is. When buying a car seat it is important to find one that is compatible with your vehicle. Each car seat has a different profile and will fit differently in different vehicles. Once you have chosen a seat, read the installation and user manual carefully and if you are unsure whether you are fitting your car seat properly, seek advice and a demonstration from a trained shop assistant. According to the National Highway Traffic Safety Administration, as many as 50–80 per cent of car seats in use today are improperly installed. This certainly contributes to many of the 9,000 accidents each year involving children travelling in a car.

There are two types of rear-facing baby seats. The first type is generally designed for babies up to 10kg (22lb), roughly from birth to six to nine months. The second type is generally for babies up to 13kg (29lb), roughly from birth to 12–15 months. Rear-facing seats provide greater protection for the baby's head, neck and spine than forward-facing seats, so it is best to keep your baby in a rear-facing seat for as long as possible. Only move him to a forward-facing seat once he has exceeded the maximum weight for the baby seat, or the top of his head is higher than the top of the seat.

The forward-facing child seat is usually designed for children weighing 9–18kg (20–40lb), roughly from nine months to four years. Only move your child to a booster seat when they have exceeded the maximum weight for the child seat, or the top of their head is higher than the top of the seat.

The booster seat is generally made for children weighing 15–25kg (33–55lb), roughly four to six years. Some booster seats are designed to be converted into a booster cushion by detaching the backrest.

The booster cushion is designed for children weighing 22–36kg (48–79lb), roughly from six to eleven years. Booster seats and booster cushions do not have an integral harness to hold the child in place. The adult seat belt goes around the child and the seat, so it is important that the seat belt is correctly adjusted. The belt should be worn as tight as possible; the lap belt should go over the pelvic region, not the stomach; the diagonal strap should rest over the shoulder, not the neck.

The placement of your child's seat in your car is also very important. All children should ride in the back seat. The centre of the back seat is the safest place for young children. It is important to note that infants in a rear-facing car seat should never ride in the front seat of a vehicle that has an air bag. Air bags were not designed to work with rear-facing infant seats, and the results in a crash can be fatal. If your car does not have a back seat and you have air bags, you must take your vehicle to the manufacturer and have them install an on/off switch for the air bag.

Check your child's seat on a regular basis to make sure all straps and cushions are in good condition and that the seat has not slipped out of place. A properly installed and maintained car seat can save your child's life. Also be sure you are following the instructions for your child's age and weight (infants and young children should ride rear-facing, older children can ride forward-facing).

Unless an adult is sitting next to the toddler in the back seat, he should not be allowed to eat or drink during the journey. If he is screaming for a drink or snack, it is better to stop the car for a few minutes than risk him choking on his food or drink, particularly if you have to break hard.

It is also important to note that the Chartered Society of Physiotherapists advises parents to avoid leaving their toddlers and children in car seats for too long, as this can delay muscle development.

Emergencies

If you have not already attended one, enlist on a first aid course so that you are able to deal with an accident if one does occur. Keep a list of emergency numbers by the phone both upstairs and downstairs and make sure that anyone who is left to look after your toddler is aware where the numbers are and also where the first aid box is. Never leave your baby with anyone who does not understand how to administer basic first aid.

Final note

I hope that the guidance and suggestions offered in this book will help you to understand, avoid and, if necessary, solve many of the common problems you may face during the second and third years of your child's life. In my first book, *The New Contented Little Baby Book*, I stressed the importance of structuring a baby's feeding and sleeping habits, as many of the problems experienced by parents of young babies are food or sleep-related, and often both. I am convinced that this is equally true of the difficulties presented by toddlers and young children. The case histories in this book, supported by the thousands of telephone calls and letters that I receive, confirm my belief that an overtired and poorly nourished child is far more likely to suffer from behavioural and sleep-related problems, such as tantrums, nightmares and jealousy, than a child who is well rested and well fed.

It is vitally important during the toddler years that your child continues to follow a regular feeding and sleeping pattern. When this routine is combined with love, encouragement and support, your child will be in the best position to embrace the many challenges he will encounter during his first three years – and you will be in the best position to delight in his successful transition from contented baby to confident child.

Further Reading

Ferber, Richard *Solve Your Child's Sleep Problems,* Dorling Kindersley 1986

Ford, Gina *The New Contented Little Baby Book,* Vermilion 2006

Ford, Gina *The Complete Sleep Guide for Contented Babies and Toddlers,* Vermilion 2006

Green, Christopher *Toddler Taming,* Vermilion 2001

Leach, Penelope *Your Baby and Child,* Penguin Books 2003

Morse, Elizabeth *My Child Won't Eat,* Penguin Books 1988

Nelsen, Jane *Positive Discipline: The First Three Years,* Prima Publishing 1998

Pearce, Professor John *The New Baby and Toddler Sleep Programme,* Vermilion 1999

Stoppard, Miriam *The New Babycare Book: A practical guide to the first three years,* Dorling Kindersley 2001

Weissbluth, Marc *Healthy Sleep Habits Happy Child,* Vermilion 2005

Index

Also by Gina Ford
Available from Vermilion

Also by Gina Ford

Available from Random House Children's Books

Introducing a brand new, bright and interactive series for babies and toddlers! The Ella and Tom series has been specially created to gently introduce little ones to new experiences and enhance their imaginations.

These touchy feely board books are ideal for babies and parents to share and children will love touching the different textures:

Ella and Tom: On the Farm
Ella and Tom: Let's Play

Perfect for little hands, these bright lift-the-flap board books encourage learning through play:

Ella and Tom: Going on a Picnic
Ella and Tom: Sleepy Time

Also available:

Gina Ford's Bedtime Songs for Contented Little Babies
A beautiful book of songs and lullabies that will help soothe your baby to sleep. Includes a CD containing over 30 minutes of tranquil songs and music, just right for helping your baby drift off at sleeptime.